FREEMASONRY AND CHRISTIANITY

Are they compatible?

A contribution to discussion

prepared by the Working Group established by the Standing Committee of the General Synod of the Church of England in the light of the motion carried by the General Synod in February 1985.

This Report has only the authority of the Working Group which prepared it.

CHURCH HOUSE PUBLISHING
Church House, Great Smith Street, London SW1P 3NZ

ISBN 0 7151 3716 6

GS 784A

Published 1987 for the General Synod of the Church of England by Church House Publishing

Contents

Acknowledgements

Permission is gratefully acknowledged for the reproduction of material from the following copyright sources:

The Evidence of the United Grand Lodge to the Working Party, dated April 1986.

Letters of the United Grand Lodge relating to the discussion and resolution of matters regarding the physical penalties of the three Craft Degrees and the Holy Royal Arch.

Canon Richard Tydeman's address to Grand Chapter, 13 November 1985.

The Leaflets *What is Freemasonry* and *Freemasonry and Religion,* United Grand Lodge of England.

Emulation Ritual, 7th edition, Lewis (Masonic Publishers) Ltd 1985.

Aldersgate Royal Arch Ritual, 10th edition, Lewis (Masonic Publishers) Ltd 1986.

The Book of Constitutions, United Grand Lodge of England 1984.

The Craft: A History of English Freemasonry, John Hamill, Crucible 1986.

The Brotherhood: The Secret World of the Freemasons, Stephen Knight, Granada Publishing Ltd 1984.

Introduction

1   At the February Group of Sessions, 1985, the General Synod passed a Private Member's Motion moved by Mr R.E.C. Clark (then a lay representative of the Diocese of Lincoln) in the following terms:

> That this Synod requests the Standing Committee to bring forward for debate a report which considers the compatibility or otherwise of Freemasonry with Christianity.

2   What was being proposed was a working group of five people meeting five times to prepare a short report costing about £800 or £1600 if account is taken of staff time (*Report of Proceedings,* vol. 16, no. 1, p.121).

3   It is also important to note that it was suggested in the course of the debate and fully accepted by the proposer of the Motion, that 'it would be a good idea if practising Freemasons were included in any working party that might be set up' (ibid., p.126).

4   The imminence of the election of a new General Synod in the Autumn of 1985 delayed the appointment of a Working Group by the Standing Committee. However, it was possible to announce at the meeting of the new General Synod on 4th February 1986 that the membership of the Working Group would be:

Dr Margaret Hewitt (Chairman)
Dr Christina Baxter
The Rev. J.C. Broadhurst
The Rev. J.C. Duxbury
Dr R.J.C. Hart
The Rev. D.R.J. Holloway
The Dean of St Albans (The Very Rev. P.C. Moore)

Dr Hart and the Dean of St. Albans had no objection to it being known that they were particularly invited as current members of Freemasonry.

5   The first brief meeting of the Working Group was held on 6th February 1986.

6   On 10th February 1986, the Secretary to the Working Group, Mr N. D. Barnett, issued a Press release inviting written evidence and asking that it be submitted to him no later than 30th April 1986.

7   As a matter of courtesy, Mr Barnett had informed the United Grand Lodge of England that the Standing Committee of the General Synod were now activating the 1985 resolution and the Grand Secretary of the United Grand Lodge issued his own Press Statement on the same day:

> Freemasons would regret that an investigation was necessary but will be pleased to know that the Grand Lodge will be invited to give evidence.

8   The Working Group was thus able to rely on the co-operation of the United Grand Lodge, an exclusively male organisation, in pursuit of their task. Unfortunately, despite two separate invitations to do so, no evidence has been submitted by the Honourable Fraternity of Ancient Freemasons, an exclusively female organisation. The Working Group therefore had to rely on press articles concerning the organisation, articles on which their Most Worshipful Master preferred to offer no comment.

9   In addition to the substantial evidence submitted by the Grand Lodge, the Working Group received 106 written submissions, of which five were from members of the General Synod. At its first meeting the Working Group agreed that all letters received should remain *entirely* confidential to the Group and to the Group alone. For this reason we have not included a list of those from whom evidence was received. Similarly we do not attribute quotations from that evidence – except in the case of the United Grand Lodge, which confirmed to us that we are free to do so.

On analysis, the number of submissions from non-Masons and Masons appeared to be fairly well-balanced. The evidence from non-Masons included some from relatives of Masons, as well as some from Masons who had either left the Craft or ceased to be active members. The evidence from active Masons was heavily weighted by the number of submissions from Church of England clergy, including some from dignitaries now mostly retired.

PREVIOUS CALLS FOR AN ENQUIRY

10   It is worth noting that, time and again, reference was made in the evidence submitted to the Working Group to the work of Walton Hannah – *Darkness Visible* (1952) and *Christian by Degrees* (1954). It was Hannah's article, 'Should a Christian be a Freemason?', published in *Theology*, January 1951, which had sparked off a debate in Church Assembly in June of that year on a motion introduced by the Rev. R. C. Meredith (Oxford), a Freemason himself, proposing:

> That, in view of the widespread publicity which has been given to the article by the Revd Walton Hannah...a Commission be appointed (including among its members persons learned in the science of Comparative Religion) to examine the statements made by Mr Hannah in that article and to report whether, in their opinion, the attention of the House of Bishops should be directed to anything therein set forth. *(Church Assembly Proceedings, vol.XXXI,1951, p.232).*

THE PRESENT ENQUIRY

12   From the outset it was evident to the present Working Group that the constraints under which they had to work – to meet five times and prepare a short paper – required them to consider how they could best serve the General Synod in meeting the expectations voiced in the 1985 debate. There was clearly concern regarding the nature of Masonic oaths; Masonic ritual; and the apparent secrecy surrounding Masonic activities. References were also made to Freemasons forming 'a mildly sinister Mafia' and to Masonry being 'the way people think it is the way to get on'.

13   Fascinating though it might have been to investigate these last allegations, the Working Group had to bear in mind that anxiety had also been expressed that their enquiry should not assume the quality of a witch-hunt. They were even more conscious of the complexity of such an investigation. If there really is a serious concern on the part of the present General Synod that such allegations be pursued effectively, and not judged by bad cases, then a larger Group, working for a longer time, equipped with research assistants, armed with legal advisers and furnished with more substantial evidence than the present Working Group have received, would be the only means of avoiding the General Synod and its agents being made to look extremely foolish. (See Appendix I)

14   The Working Group have also been very wary of making categorical assertions regarding the actual provenance of initiation texts used by Freemasons. Mr Clark himself acknowledged that they would be 'a lifetime's work'; a study which undoubtedly would call for considerable work by those few people who are acknowledged as genuinely expert in the field of comparative religion, none of whom are among the membership of the present Working Group nor in the ranks of the General Synod.

15   As their contribution to informed discussion of the compatibility of Freemasonry with Christianity the Working Group submit to the General Synod a paper which includes:

(a) a brief historical background to modern Freemasonry in England
(b) comments on its constitution and structure
(c) analysis of the nature of the "secrecy" of the organisation
(d) an examination of the rituals of the three Craft Degrees and of the Holy Royal Arch (but see Appendix II)
(e) an exploration of the nature and the extent of Masonic charity.

The Historical Background of Freemasonry in England

16 The literature on the origins and development of Freemasonry in England is extensive. Although detailed examination of it lies outside the scope of the Working Group's particular task, it is nevertheless important to note that few modern commentators claim to certain knowledge of its history earlier than 1717. Walton Hannah, writing in 1954, observed:

> We may dismiss out of hand the lunatic fringe of fantasiasts who profess to trace a direct historical continuity between the Craft today and King Solomon, or the Druids, the mysteries of ancient Egypt, of Eleusis, of Dionysius(*sic*), or any other ancient system. If modern Masons...have claimed that Freemasonry is the steward and guardian of ancient mysteries of which it is the legitimate heir, all that can be conceded to them is that there are indeed striking parallels and resemblances even in the actual signs and symbols; symbolism, however, is an exceedingly vague subject on which to be dogmatic and precise, and as ancient mysteries and religions had many points in common even where no common ancestor can be traced, it is hardly remarkable that the Masonic mysteries today should also show similarities to them. *(Christian by Degrees, p.23).*

Hannah went on to dismiss other theories which relate Freemasonry to the Knights Templar and readily conceded that allegations concerning the influence of Rosicrucianism on Freemasonry have 'been pushed to quite ridiculous extremes' (ibid., p.24).

17 More recently, John Hamill, Librarian and Curator of the Grand Lodge Library and Museum, has written of theories of the origin of Freemasonry:

> When, Why and Where did Freemasonry originate? There is one answer to these questions: we do not know, despite all the paper and ink that has been expended in examining them. Indeed, the issues have been greatly clouded by well-meaning but ill-informed Masonic historians themselves. *(The Craft, p.15).*

We do know, however, that Lodges very much like modern Lodges existed in the seventeenth century; that on 24th June 1717 the Grand

Lodge of England was formed; that a rival Antients Grand Lodge was formally constituted in 1751; and that these two rival Grand Lodges joined together on 27th December 1813 to form the United Grand Lodge of England, much as we know it today.

18   Two questions relating to the emergence of modern Freemasonry and directly relevant to the task of the Working Group are:

(a) in what sense was it a secret organisation?
       and
(b) was it a Christian organisation?

19   Any competent social historian will be familiar with the fact that secret societies were very much the fashion in seventeenth-century England. Some were the inevitable product of a society intolerant of nonconformity in religion and politics, others seem to have been formed by men attracted by a contemporary fascination for the occult.

20   By 1676, Freemasonry was well enough known to be worth lampooning in the Press, The Freemasons themselves appear to have been little concerned to conceal their existence. Indeed, between 1721 and 1747, the Annual Assembly and Feast of the premier Grand Lodge in London was a very public occasion:

> The brethren all met at the town house of the incoming noble Grand Master and a procession, preceded and followed by bands of musicians, was formed to march from there to the hall where the Festival was to take place. The brethren would march two by two dressed in their aprons and jewels, and carrying the emblems, symbols, and banners of the Craft, followed by the nobility in their carriages and chariots. *(The Craft, p.77).*

Not surprisingly such processions attracted public attention with the result that a regulation was made in April 1747 that in future 'no public procession of masons cloathed in the badges of the Order' could be held without dispensation' (ibid.).

21   That dispensations were given and that Freemasons continued to advertise their presence in a town throughout the eighteenth and nineteenth centuries, however, is well attested by the regular reports carried by provincial newspapers of public processions by local lodges, often going to divine service, or of the public processions of the Provincial Grand Lodge, again usually going to Church. As well as in their own processions, lodges would take part, in regalia, in processions as part of local or national celebrations. (ibid., p.84).

22   The "secrecy" of Freemasonry thus scarcely lay in a covert existence. Rather it lay then – as it lies now – in the strict privacy of its
Lodge meetings; in the exclusiveness of its membership; and the special
emphasis placed on the solemn pledges required of initiates never to
divulge the words and signs by which they recognised their fellow members of the Craft. Then as now, it was these features which not merely
engendered suspicion but drew down outright condemnation of their
activities. The pamphlet *To All Godly People in the City of London* (1698)
urges its readers to:

> ...take care lest their Ceremonies and secret swearings take hold of you: and
> be wary that none cause you to err from Godliness. For this devlish Sect of
> Men are Meeters in Secret..For how should Men meet in Secret Places and
> with secret Signes taking care that none observe them to do the Work of
> God...? *(The Craft,* pp.37-8).

23   In the early years of the eighteenth century, public reference was
being made to the 'Signes and Tokens' of Freemasonry and, from 1723
onwards, there were a series of exposures of the rituals and secrets of the
Craft.

24   The "secrets" of Freemasonry remain to this day the signs, grips
and words used in proof of membership. They are generally said to have
been derived from or modelled on the ways and means by which members of medieval stonemasons' guilds, itinerant members of a skilled
craft, recognised each other and were able to attest to their skill – a sort
of medieval certificate of professional competence and a means of
detecting impostors. As were the medieval craftsmen, so the initiate to
Freemasonry is required to swear never to reveal his "secrets" to non-
Masons.

25   Just why these customs were adopted as a basis for a new organisation in the seventeenth century, when effective craft organisation
with the apprenticeship system on which it relied was already a dying
institution, is very far from clear. Certainly it would be an interesting
field for further historical research. Stephen Knight may be as percep-
tive as any when he suggests that it

> stemmed from curiosity, antiquarian interest, and a kind of fashionable
> search for an unconventional, exclusive social milieu – rather like a jet-set
> fad for frequenting working men's pubs...There were thus cosmopolitan
> romance, an exclusivity and an organised secretiveness about the mason's
> guild...All of this had potential fascination for men of education. *(The
> Brotherhood* pp.17-18).

7

Be this as it may, the use in Masonic ritual of archaic language and the adoption of medieval practices, embellished in the early eighteenth century by the introduction of blood-curdling oaths and dire penalties, proved a source not merely of curiosity but of a constant suspicion as to the nature and objects of Freemasonry which has persisted to the present day.

A CHRISTIAN SOCIETY?

26   From the time of the Union of the Grand Lodge of England and the Antients Grand Lodge, the answer is clearly "No". References to the Supreme Being in the original Masonic rituals seem undoubtedly to have been to the God of the Christian faith. In 1816, in the hope of enabling men of different faiths to take part in Lodge rituals without offending or compromising their own belief, specifically Christian references were largely removed from Craft rituals in England. In fact, during the eighteenth century, the Grand Lodge of England had itself been much engaged in reconstructing some of its rituals. One man who played a prominent part in this work was Dr James Anderson, a Scottish minister, whose first versions of his proposed *Constitutions* was presented to the Grand Master in 1723. In his proposed new 'Charges of a Freemason', the first had the most far-reaching consequences:

> Tis now thought more expedient only to oblige them [members of the Brotherhood] to that Religion which all men agree, leaving their particular opinions to themselves. (Quoted by Knight, op.cit., p.27).

27   On the union of the two rival Grand Lodges in 1813, the Antients, who emphasised a link with Christianity, gave way to the Moderns (the Grand Lodge) and accepted their, by then established, practice of omitting specific references to Christ or the Christian faith and thereafter the only – but essential – demand made of those wishing to enter the Craft was and remains that they had a belief in God.

> 'Let a man's religion or mode of worship be what it may, he is not excluded from the order, provided he believes in the glorious architect of heaven and earth, and practise the sacred duties of morality'. (i.e. what may be called a "comprehensive attitude towards religions" was established.) (*Grand Lodge 1717 – 1967*, UGL 1967, p.213).

The Organisation and Structure of Freemasonry in England

(See para. 8 above and also Appendix III)

28   Basic Craft Freemasonry is organised in 'Lodges': groups of Freemasons who meet regularly together and are under the jurisdiction of the United Grand Lodge of England. In 1985, there was 8,253 such Lodges and some 320,000 members (statistics of membership need to be handled with some care since individual Freemasons may be members of more than one Lodge). It is the Grand Lodge alone that has the power to expel errant members from the Craft although Provincial and District Grand Masters or, as regards the London Lodges, the Board of Purposes have power to suspend a member.

29   It is the Grand Lodge, again, which is the sole authority for the 'recognition' of other Grand Lodges in other parts of the world provided they satisfy certain basic principles of English Freemasonry which, according to the evidence submitted to the Working Party by Grand Lodge itself, include requirements that:

(a)   their members believe in a Supreme Being
(b)   the Bible be open at every Masonic meeting. When there are non-Christian members present the Volume of the Sacred Law of their own religion be also open
(c)   the discussion of religion and politics be prohibited in Lodges
(d)   membership be exclusively male.

To be recognised, a Grand Lodge must also be sovereign, i.e. it must have jurisdiction over basic Freemasonry in its territory and must not in any way be subject to the authority of another Masonic body. Grand Lodges which cease to follow these principles become irregular and recognition is withdrawn, as, for example, the United Grand Lodge withdrew recognition from the Grand Lodge in Belgium in 1979 when it ceased to insist that its members believe in a Supreme Being. (The United Grand Lodge listed Grand Lodges it currently recognises and this list is reproduced as Appendix IV.)

30   It is curious that, in this part of their evidence and elsewhere, reference is made by the United Grand Lodge to the essential require- ment of Freemasons that they believe in *a* Supreme Being. In the course of the present century, the United Grand Lodge has felt it desirable to issue public statements clarifying the aims and relationships of the Craft (cf. Appendix V). In all three, 1920, 1938 and 1949, reference is made not to a belief in *a* but *the* Supreme Being and it is a belief in *the* Supreme Being that is required in the second of 'those Basic Principles of Freemasonry for which the Grand Lodge of England has stood throughout its history' (*Information for the Guidance of Members of the Craft*, p.3) and the printed United Grand Lodge of England *Constitutions* insist:

> That a belief in the G(reat) A(rchitect) O(f) T(he) U(niverse) and His revealed will shall be an essential qualification for membership.

31   This second Principle is in fact a conflation of the first of *the Antient Charges of a Free-Mason:*

> 1. Concerning GOD and RELIGION
> A Mason is obliged, by his tenure, to obey the moral law; and if he rightly understand the art he will never be a stupid atheist nor an irreligious liber- tine. He, of all men, should best understand that God seeth not as man seeth; for man looketh at the outward appearance, but God looketh to the heart. A mason is, therefore, particularly bound never to act against the dic- tates of his conscience. Let a man's religion or mode of worship be what it may, he is not excluded from the order, provided he believe in the glorious architect of heaven and earth, and practise the sacred duties of morality. (*Constitutions*, p.3)

The legitimacy of the apparent assumption that the God of each and all religions can be encapsulated in the all-embracing concept of the Great Architect will be discussed later in this Report.

MEMBERSHIP

32   The rules for the election of those wishing to be initiated into membership of a Lodge are set out very clearly in the *Constitutions* of the United Grand Lodge, a book available to the general public. Every applicant is required to complete a form of application approved by the Board of General Purposes of the Grand Lodge and supplied by its Grand Secretary. He is required to state full name, age, profession or occupation (if any), place or places of abode, business address or addresses, and the names of his proposer and seconder (Rule 164). The

candidate must be personally known to his proposer and seconder, who must themselves be members of the Lodge and able to state that he is a man of good reputation and well fitted to become a member of the Lodge (Rule 159). An applicant may not actually be known personally to all members of the Lodge. It is the business of the Lodge Committee, who meet to vet all applications for membership, to arrange for such a man to be interviewed by one of their number, just as would be the case if he were applying for membership of a London Club. Election depends on a ballot at a regular meeting of the Lodge, which in England is by the use of black and white balls:

> No person shall be made a Mason in, or admitted a member of, a Lodge, if, on the ballot, three black balls appear against him: but the by-laws of a Lodge may enact that two black balls or one black ball shall exclude a candidate...(Rule 165).

An elected candidate may be initiated on the day of his election but must be initiated within a year of election, otherwise the election is void.

APPLICATION NOT INVITATION

33   Rule 162 requires of every candidate that, before his initiation, he sign a declaration:

> To the Master, Wardens, Officers and Members of the Lodge of ......No.......
> I, ..., being a free man, and of the full age of twenty-one years, do declare that, unbiassed by the improper solicitation of friends, and uninfluenced by mercenary or other unworthy motive, I do freely and voluntarily offer myself a candidate for the mysteries of Masonry; that I am prompted by a favourable opinion conceived of the institution, and a desire of knowledge; and that I will cheerfully conform to all the antient usages and the established customs of the Order.
>
> Witness my hand, this......of......
>
> Witness......

34   The claim that Freemasons never invite men to join, but all have to apply, needs to be qualified. The booklet *Information for the Guidance of Members of the Craft*, which is given to every new Mason on his initiation, includes (p.22) a special section on:

> SOLICITATION OF CANDIDATES FOR FREEMASONRY
> The question of improper solicitation of candidates has been raised on many occasions and the Board feels that a statement on this matter would be helpful to the Craft.

11

There is no objection to a neutrally worded approach being made to a man who is considered a suitable candidate for Freemasonry. There can be no objection to his being reminded, once, that the approach was made. The potential candidate should then be left to make his own decision, without further solicitation. (Extract from Report of Board of General Purposes adopted 9 December 1981)

Few would dispute that many men have joined the Craft at the suggestion of their friends or colleagues. Nevertheless, all candidates at their initiation are required to state that they come of their own free will.

INITIATION AND REGISTRATION

35   On initiation, the newly admitted Mason must pay the initiation fee prescribed by his Lodge in its by-laws. Every initiation has to be notified to the Grand Secretary of the United Grand Lodge, who will enter the name of the newly admitted Mason on the Register of the Grand Lodge and who will, if applied to in due form, issue a Certificate to that effect. (Rule 174). The Grand Secretary has also to be informed each year of the effective membership of every Lodge. (Rule 146).

THE THREE 'CRAFT' DEGREES OF FREEMASONRY

36   On initiation, the new Mason becomes an 'Entered Apprentice'. Four weeks later, and after further instruction in the Craft, he may be 'passed' with further ritual into the Second Degree as 'a Fellow Craft'. Four weeks later again, and after more instruction and with further ritual, he may be 'raised' to the Third Degree of 'Master Mason'. Theoretically it is possible for a man to be initiated, passed and raised within eight weeks, but in how many instances this is actually the case is not known to the Working Group.

These three degrees account for most of the membership of 'the Craft'. It has been suggested that only one in three Freemasons takes any further degree, although there are many others, including the so-called Higher Degrees. (cf. *Darkness Visible* pp. 197-209).

THE HOLY ROYAL ARCH

37   This was originally a separate degree, but came to be seen as the 'completion' of the degree of Master Mason at the unification of the Grand Lodge of England with the Antients in 1813, although it is under the separate control of the Grand Chapter, not the Grand Lodge, both

of whom operate from Freemasons' Hall in London. The *Information* booklet contains (p.17) a reminder that 'the Master Mason's degree includes the Supreme Order of the Holy Royal Arch' and recommends that Master Masons 'should be encouraged in their Lodges to complete their Third Degree by seeking exaltation in a Royal Arch Chapter' which is technically possible four weeks after taking the Third Degree: and it is possible for the same men to be officers of both (*Christian by Degrees*, p.74).

THE SO-CALLED HIGHER DEGREES (THE ANTIENT AND ACCEPTED RITE)

38   These, known to the United Grand Lodge as 'Further Degrees', from Secret Master to Grand Inspector General are governed by their own Supreme Council housed in Duke Street, St James'. In marked contrast to initiation into the three Craft Degrees, which has to be sought, initiation into any of these degrees is only open to Master Masons who are selected by the Supreme Council. According to Stephen Knight:

> only a small proportion, even of the limited number of Freemasons who take the first step [beyond the Third Degree], progress beyond the 18th Degree, that of Knight of the Pelican and Eagle and Sovereign Prince Rose Croix of Heredom. With each Degree, the number of initiates diminishes. The 31st Degree (Grand Inspector Inquisitor Commander) is restricted to 400 members; the 32nd (Sublime Prince of the Royal Secret) to 180; and the 33rd – the pre-eminent Grand Inspectors General – to only 75 members. (*The Brotherhood,* p.41)

39   Unlike the three Craft Degrees and the Holy Royal Arch, only a few of the Higher Degrees are conferred by special ritual in this country. The 4th to 17th Degrees are conferred at once and in name only during the initiation of the selected Freemason to the 18th Degree. For the few who rise higher than the 18th Degree, the 19th to 29th are conferred nominally during the rite of initiation to the 30th Degree – that of the Grand Elected Knight Kadosh or Knight of the Black and White Eagle. Degrees above the 30th are conferred singly. No initiate can rise higher than the 18th Degree without the unanimous agreement of the entire Supreme Council. (Cf. Appendix VI)

13

A 'Secret' Society?

40   Many are concerned by the secrecy of Freemasonry: 'if Freemasonry is right, why all the secrecy?' asks Andy Arbuthnot (*Should a Christian be a Freemason?*) and many others. In their evidence to the Working Group, the United Grand Lodge argued very strongly that the element of secrecy was much exaggerated by their detractors, making the point that Freemasonry, historically, has been exempted from legislation suppressing secret societies considered a danger to the state. They add a number of other, perhaps more immediately relevant, points:

> Freemasons are under no obligation to conceal their membership of the Craft...

> The meeting places of Freemasons' Lodges are not hidden. They may not always be labelled as such, but the neighbourhood will know, and there is usually some external indication of the building's purpose, even if it is only a decorative Square and Compasses. Some (e.g. Freemasons' Hall in London) are open to the public.

> The aims of Freemasonry have been published in the press.

> Freemasonry's rule book, the Book of Constitutions (which also states its aims) is available for purchase by any member of the public.

> The affairs of its Lodges are private, as are the internal affairs of other private associations or clubs.

They concluded their submission on this particular matter by re-asserting that 'the secrets of Freemasonry are the signs, grips and words used in proof of membership'.

41   Very early in the life of the Working Group it became clear that even these 'secrets' are pretty open secrets and have been for many years.

42   The Grand Lodge itself is inhibited and inhibits its members from making such revelations. *Information for the Guidance of Members of the Craft* is quite explicit on this point:

MASONIC SECRETS

In view of the increasing number of publications purporting or affecting to give particulars of the secrets and inner proceedings of the Craft, the Board desires to notify that the preparation, publication, sale, or circulation of such works is a Masonic offence, and that when reported and proved, the offending Brother will be dealt with by disciplinary methods. The Board would add a strong warning to Brethren generally to be extremely cautious in any allusions, whether spoken, written or printed, to Masonic matters which may thus come into the possession of unqualified persons.

43   Paradoxically, the Working Group had no difficulty whatsoever in obtaining copies of the *Emulation Ritual,* one of the several 'workings' of Lodges under the Grand Lodge of England. The Emulation Lodge of Improvement itself operates under a committee, all of whose members are senior, *bona fide* Freemasons, and its version of Masonic 'workings' is recognised and authenticated in its submission to the Grand Lodge. This proved only one of several paradoxes of Freemasonry the Working Group were to notice.

44   Nevertheless an essential feature of the rituals of Craft Masonry is that the candidate undertakes 'without evasion, equivocation, or mental reservation of any kind', never to reveal to a non-Mason any of the steps, signs and grips and words which are disclosed to a candidate in the initiation ceremony, the ceremonies of Passing from the Degree of Entered Apprentice to that of Fellow Craft and Raising from Fellow Craft to that of Master Mason. 'The marks by which we are known to each other and distinguished from the rest of the world' should not be revealed to non-Masons.

45   Seeking admission to the Royal Holy Arch, the candidate not only swears that he

> will always hele, conceal, and never divulge any of the secrets or mysteries restricted to this Supreme Degree, denominated the Holy Royal Arch of Jerusalem, to anyone in the world unless it be a true and lawful Companion of the Order whom I shall find to be such after strict examination.

He also solemnly promises

> that I will not dare to pronounce that Sacred and Mysterious Name which may now for the first time be communicated to me, unless in the presence and with the assistance of two or more Royal Arch Companions, or in the body of a lawfully constituted Royal Arch Chapter, whilst acting as First Principal.

46   In *Darkness Visible*, however, Hannah published the full rituals of the first three Masonic Degrees and of the Royal Arch; the accuracy of his account remains unchallenged and is agreed by the Grand Lodge. Hannah's book has gone through fifteen impressions and more than 50,000 copies and still sells steadily. The *Emulation Ritual* itself was first published in 1969. Stephen Knight's *The Brotherhood*, which in an Appendix gives a brief account of the initiation ritual of the First Degree, appeared in 1984 and was reprinted nine times in that year alone. Any good library will have yet other books which contain or explain the "Secrets" of Freemasonry. Yet Craft members continue to swear a solemn oath on the Bible not to reveal secrets, which are not secrets at all!

47   This, to a non-Mason, may appear more than a little odd, even farcical, but one Freemason wrote to the Working Group that the 'secrets' are regarded as signs and tokens, as symbolic: 'they represent something deeper – that bond of brotherhood, which only those who are Freemasons can understand. In other words, what is sworn to is fidelity and friendship towards his fellow-Masons'.

48   However, the traditional penalties for breaking the oaths, for revealing the 'secrets' of the Craft, have been a matter of some anxiety in Masonic circles for many years. They are spelled out in the Obligations which until recently (see para. 53) candidates were invited to undertake for admission to the three Craft Degrees and for installation as the Worshipful Master of a Lodge.

> These several points I solemnly swear to observe, without evasion, equivocation, or mental reservation of any kind, under no less a penalty, on the violation of any of them than that of having my throat cut across, my tongue torn out by the root, and buried in the sand of the sea at low water mark, or a cable's length from the shore, where the tide regularly ebbs and flows twice in twenty-four hours, or the more effective punishment of being branded as a wilfully perjured individual, void of all moral worth, and totally unfit to be received into this worshipful Lodge...(First Degree).

Again:

> These several points I solemnly swear to observe, without evasion, equivocation, or mental reservation of any kind, under no less a penalty, on the violation of any of them, than that of having my left breast laid open, my heart torn therefrom, and given to the ravenous birds of the air, or devouring beasts of the field as prey...(Second Degree).

Or again:

All these points I solemnly swear to observe, without evasion, equivocation, or mental reservation of any kind, under no less a penalty, on the violation of any of them, than that of being severed in two, my bowels burned to ashes, and those ashes scattered over the face of the earth, and wafted by the four cardinal winds of heaven, that no trace or remembrance of so vile a wretch may longer be found among men, particularly Master Masons (Third Degree).

In the case of the installation of the Worshipful Master, the penalty for revealing the secrets of the Lodge was:

to have the right hand struck off and slung over the left shoulder, there to wither and decay.

The penalty attaching to the obligation at the ceremony of Exaltation to Royal Arch Masonry was 'that of suffering the loss of life by having my head struck off'.

It is difficult to reconcile these extravagant oaths with the dominical injunction in the Sermon on the Mount to 'swear not at all' and to 'let what you say be simply 'Yes' or 'No'' (Matt. 5. 33-37). As for the barbaric penalties invoked, honoured more in the breach than in the observance, they were an abuse of language.

49   The present Grand Master first voiced his misgivings about the physical penalties as long ago as 1979, when, addressing the Grand Lodge at the Annual Investiture of that year, he said:

I remember feeling a very definite sensation of repugnance when I came to repeat the penalties clause in its old form.

He went on to refer to 'the distasteful aspect of calling upon God to witness an Oath which is scarcely practical and certainly barbarous'. He referred to the matter again when presiding at the Quarterly Communication of the Grand Lodge in March 1985:

It seems to me that it would not be a very radical step, and would in no way affect the meaning of the Ritual, if the penalties were removed entirely from the Obligations, and treated as a form of traditional history.

50   Twenty years earlier, a discussion of the matter had been raised by Bishop Herbert, a prominent Freemason himself, as a consequence of which a 'permissive variation' was allowed (and subsequently printed in *Emulation Ritual)* in which the Obligations were changed to indicate that reference to the penalties was traditional, not an indication of practice.

51   Not surprisingly, the nature of the Obligations has been a feature

of Masonic ritual to which public attention has been drawn and one of the reasons why Freemasonry has been condemned by its critics, who remained unimpressed by the conventional defence that, in any case, the penalties were never taken literally; that they are clearly symbolic. The very fact that they were undertaken with the candidate's hand on the open Bible has always added weight to such criticism. 'If it [the oath] is not taken seriously', wrote Canon Demant to Walton Hannah, 'or taken very symbolically (in contravention of the oath's words: without evasion, equivocation, or mental reservation of any kind) then the oath comes under the heading of vain swearing or profanity. If it is taken seriously, then it must be put down as rash swearing ...' (*Darkness Visible,* p.24).

52   There can be no doubt that the Grand Lodge has been sensitive on the matter of the physical penalties. 'The existence of the physical penalties ... gives ready material for attack by our enemies and detractors', the Board of General Purposes observed in its 'Report on the Penalties in the Obligations' in 1986. It was the last but probably not the least of their reasons for proposing a resolution for the approval of the Grand Lodge in June of that year that 'all references to physical penalties be omitted from the Obligations taken by Candidates in the three Degrees and by a Master Elect at his Installation but retained [i.e. referred to in detail] elsewhere in the respective ceremonies'. Indeed, specific reference to the traditional penalties in other parts of the ceremonies is necessary to give meaning to the 'signs' of the Degrees.

53   The Grand Master wished it 'to be clearly understood that any change ... will be of our making, and not because people outside Freemasonry have suggested it'. Whatever the reason for the change, the Resolution was in fact approved by a large majority of the Grand Lodge, which exercised its powers to direct that the necessary alterations to the rituals be put into effect as soon as possible and in any event not later than June 1987 (cf. Appendix VII).

54   Members of the General Synod will be interested in the arguments in favour of the change advanced in the Report of the Board of General Purposes which, because of the importance of the change, are reproduced in full in Appendix VIII. But the change does not and cannot wholly meet all criticism of the Obligations, since it remains a fact that candidates are still required never to reveal 'secrets' the nature of which has not yet been revealed to them.

55   There is no gainsaying the fact that, since it is perfectly possible for any man wishing to become a Freemason to read up on the Craft before applying for membership, he need not necessarily be unaware of the nature and character of Freemasonry. It is certainly not correct to claim that 'a candidate [is] required to join before he *can* [our italics] find out what he has joined' (Arbuthnot, op.cit.). Nevertheless, the rituals of Initiation, and indeed of Passing and Raising, are certainly based on an assumption of ignorance and the Working Group are led to believe that candidates are not encouraged to get their subject up before applying for membership of the Craft. It is assumed that the integrity of Freemasonry is guaranteed by the integrity of those they already know to be members.

56   It is the assumption of ignorance which prompts the question: Is it right to expect Christians to swear on the open Bible that they will not reveal the 'secrets' of an organisation whose rituals clearly state that they will only be revealed when the candidate has accepted the Obligations of membership? It is on these grounds that Canon Demant concluded his observations on the Obligations: 'there is no certainty that the Christian initiate will not find afterwards that he has joined an alien cult' (*Darkness Visible*, p.24).

WHAT IS FREEMASONRY?

57   Canon Demant's observation immediately prompts the questions, What are men applying to join? What is the nature of this organisation whose Obligations they are invited to accept? These are questions easier to pose than to answer simply. Hamill (*The Craft*, p.12) writes: 'To attempt to define Freemasonry succinctly is an almost impossible task ... As there is no offical dogma, and because an individual Freemason's response to his Freemasonry is an intensely personal one, it is almost certain that if six members were asked to define what Freemasonry was to them six differing answers would result'.

In August 1985, the Grand Lodge authorised the publication of a leaflet *What Every Candidate Should Know*, which opens with the statement:

> Freemasonry is a society of men historically linked with medieval operative Masons, from whom they derive their private means of recognition, their ceremonial, and many of their customs. Its members adhere to ancient principles of Brotherly love, relief and truth not only among themselves but also in their relations with the world at large, and by ritual, precept and example.

Hamill glosses this:

> The candidate for initiation learns very early in his masonic career that the basic principles of Freemasonry are Brotherly Love, Relief and Truth. *Brotherly Love* in its sense of the promotion of tolerance and respect for the beliefs and ideals of others, and the building of a world in which that respect and tolerance, together with kindness and understanding, can flourish. *Relief* not in the limited sense of monetary giving but in the widest sense of charitable giving of money, time, and effort to assist the community as a whole. *Truth* in the sense of striving for high moral standards and in conducting one's life – in all its aspects – in as honest a manner as possible. In simple terms a Freemason is taught his duties to his God, his fellow man, and the laws of his country. (*The Craft*, p.12)

58   What is quite clear is that Masons emphatically deny that Freemasonry is a religion. A leaflet *Freemasonry and Religion*, published by the Board of General Purposes of the United Grand Lodge in 1985, states: 'Freemasonry is not a religion, nor is it a substitute for religion.' 'Freemasonry lacks the basic elements of religion' but 'is far from indifferent to religion. Without interfering in religious practice it expects each member to follow his own faith, and to place above all other duties his duty to his God by whatever name He is known …. Freemasonry is thus a supporter of religion.' In their evidence to the Working Group the United Grand Lodge further stated: 'Freemasonry knows that its rituals do not amount to the practice of religion …'

59   What are we to make of these claims on behalf of an organisation whose activities are centred on 'temples'; whose rituals contain reference to 'altars'? Why is it necessary for each Lodge to have a chaplain – albeit he need not be in Holy Orders? Is there substance in the claim that Freemasonry with its concept of the G A O T U represents or connives at a syncretistic understanding of religion and representation of God?

60   There is no way in which any responsible answer can be suggested to such questions from non-Masons without reading Masonic rituals themselves. Even then, the assessment of differing interpretations is a peculiar difficulty. How far can we agree that Freemasons are entitled to expect their own interpretation to be accepted and how far, to quote the judge in a recent libel action, are we to prefer 'the interpretation put on words as they are understood by the common man' or, in this case, by the non-Mason?

The Masonic Rituals

61   It has to be recognised that Freemasons and non-Masons alike experience some difficulty in giving an accurate interpretation of current Masonic ritual in the almost total absence of substantial evidence of the reasoning lying behind its development and elaboration in the eighteenth and nineteenth centuries. This will become only too apparent when the Royal Arch Ritual is discussed later in this Report. Conscious of their obligation not to publicise the secrets and proceedings of Freemasonry, neither the Lodge of Promulgation (authorised by the premier Grand Lodge in 1809 to examine the differences between its own rituals and those of the Antients Grand Lodge) nor the Lodge of Reconciliation (authorised after the Union to complete the reconciliation of the two systems and bring about a standard form of ritual) committed their deliberations to paper.

62   'As the revisions of the Lodge of Reconciliation were not officially written down and not allowed to be published the new system was passed on by demonstration and word of mouth' (*The Craft*, p.67). It needs little imagination to envisage the differences and divergences of intention, and obfuscation of interpretation this could lead to! Grand Lodge took so strongly the view that no attempt should be made to commit to print the rituals it approved in 1816 and 1827 that it was not until the 1870s that printed books of rituals began to become generally accepted. As has been noted earlier (para. 46) it was not until 1969 that the Emulation Lodge of Improvement (which since 1823 has been concerned, first by lectures and later by demonstration, to ensure the practice of an approved Ritual form without permitting alteration) first published its own Emulation Ritual (*Emulation Ritual* 1985, pp.13-16).

63   When, therefore, Emulation Lodge itself comments 'It may well be thought that our ritual proceedings should, periodically, be brought up to date' (ibid., p.13), one has to ask not only In what respects and for what reason?, but also What was the interpretation placed on the old rituals by the original United Grand Lodge which originally prompted them to give their approval? These are questions which it is difficult to answer since it is not certain precisely what *was* approved – or why!

64   The rituals themselves are allegorical dramas based on the partly factual, partly fictional history of King Solomon's temple; the work of Hiram Abiff 'its chief architect' and the Master Mason in command of the construction of the temple; the story of his murder; and, in the Holy Royal Arch ritual, the discovery in the foundations of his ruined temple of the 'omnific word' – the lost name of God. Each ceremony lasts about an hour and is delivered from memory – no mean feat!

65   The intended teaching of the ceremonies is briefly:

(a) Admission as an Entered Apprentice: man's natural equality and dependence on others; his civil and moral duties

(b) Passing to the degree of Fellow Craft: the study of Nature and Science; the rewards of labour

(c) Raising as a Master Mason: contemplation of inevitable death; fidelity; duty to others

(d) Admission as a Companion in the Royal Arch: awareness of man's relationship to God

(e) Installation as Master of a Lodge: duty to administer and teach.

66   The origins of the rituals cannot be dealt with quite so briefly, not least because of the problems referred to in paras. 61, 62 and 63. However we have some insight from the 'Explanation of the First Degree Tracing Board' given in *Emulation Ritual*:

> The usage and customs among Freemasons have ever borne a near affinity to those of the Ancient Egyptians. Their philosophers, unwilling to expose their mysteries to vulgar eyes, couched systems of learning and polity under signs and hieroglyphical figures, which were communicated to their chief priests or Magi alone, who were bound by solemn oath to conceal them. The system of Pythagoras was founded on a similar principle, as well as many others of more recent date.

This is interesting as a gloss on the answer given by a candidate for Passing to the question 'What is Freemasonry?': 'A peculiar system of morality, veiled in allegory and illustrated by symbols' (*Emulation Ritual*, pp. 107-8). Its emphasis comes as some surprise to those more familiar with the view that, originally, Masonic ritual in England had specifically Christian overtones.

67   The re-enactment of ancient ceremonies is, of course, not unique to Freemasonry. Bardic Circles are regularly involved in doing this. Nor is Masonic ritual unique in being syncretistic – a word perhaps

more generally feared by Masons and non-Masons alike than clearly understood. But the questions most often asked about them are, Do these rituals add up to a form of worship? If so, what is the nature of the God to whom it is directed? Is Freemasonry in fact and effect a religion?

68   In the evidence submitted to the Working Group by the Grand Lodge, it is explicitly stated that 'there is no worship involved in Masonic rituals'. The Working Group find this impossible to accept in the light of the evidence of *Emulation Ritual*:

(a)   In the Opening of the First Degree the assistance of the G A O T U is explicitly invoked:

> let us invoke the assistance of the Great Architect of the Universe in all our undertakings...Brethren, in the name of the Great Architect of the Universe I declare the Lodge duly open...

(b)   There is a prayer (headed as such) in the *Emulation Ritual* for the First Degree:

> Vouchsafe Thine aid, Almighty Father and Supreme Governor of the Universe, to our present convention, and grant that this Candidate for Freemasonry may so dedicate and devote his life to Thy service as to become a true and faithful brother among us. Endue him with a competency of Thy divine wisdom, that, assisted by the secrets of our Masonic art, he may the better be enabled to unfold the beauties of true godliness, to the honour and glory of Thy Holy Name.

(c)   In the Second Degree, there are references to 'the help of God' and 'the blessing of Heaven'; there is an actual *Prayer:*

> We supplicate the continuance of Thine aid, O merciful Lord, on behalf of ourselves and him who kneels before Thee. May the work begun in Thy Name be continued to Thy Glory and evermore established in us by obedience to Thy precepts.

(d)   In the Third Degree, the help of God and the blessing of Heaven are invoked and again prayers are addressed to:

> Almighty and Eternal God, Architect and Ruler of the Universe, at Whose creative fiat all things first were made.

69   What is specially noticeable, and for some who submitted evidence specially objectionable, about some of the phrases and prayers incorporated into the rituals, is the incorporation of familiar Christian prayers and phrases denuded of their normal Christian reference. For example, in the ritual of the Third Degree, the Worshipful Master

implores 'Almighty and Eternal God, Architect and Ruler of the Universe…to pour down on this convocation assembled in Thy Holy Name the continual dew of Thy blessing'. The Opening Ceremony of the Aldersgate Ritual for the Royal Arch actually commences with a prayer even more familiar: 'Omnipotent God, unto whom all hearts are open, all desires known, and from whom no secrets are hid, cleanse the thoughts of our hearts by the inspiration of Thy Holy Spirit, that we may perfectly love Thee and worthily magnify Thy Holy Name'. But then the words "through Christ our Lord" are omitted. The same ceremony is closed with the words 'Glory be to God on High – On earth, peace – Goodwill towards men' with no reference to the Gospel from which the words are derived. Christian opponents of Freemasonry frequently assert that this conscious and deliberate exclusion of a reference to Jesus Christ in the rituals is at the heart of their claim that Freemasonry is incompatible with Christianity.

70   Freemasons firmly reject the suggestion that not merely the *absence,* but the *deletion,* of the name of Christ from their rituals constitutes a denial of him. 'As Freemasonry is not a religion or a substitute for it, there is no reason why the name of Christ should be mentioned in its rituals' (evidence from the United Grand Lodge). It could just as reasonably be argued that, this being the case, it is unwise, to say the least, to pluck phrases and prayers from undeniable and recognisable Christian liturgies. The identification of the one with the other is too natural, and too misleading in the light of Freemasonry's claim that its rituals 'do not amount to the practice of religion'.

71   Of course there is nothing unusual in attaching different meanings to the same word, but on any definition "worship" is clearly taken to mean homage or honour paid to God. There is something very confusing, and indeed confused, about the insistence that Masonic ritual does not contain any element of worship: 'prayers in Masonic context are not acts of worship but the simple asking for a blessing at the beginning of work and returning thanks at its successful conclusion.' But prayers in Freemasonry are integral to the Rituals; is this therefore not rather a Humpty-Dumpty use of language? In ordinary usage, can such prayer be distinguished from worship?

72   Even if, for the sake of argument, such a distinction were possible, there are many who would press the point that prayers from which all reference to Christ have been deliberately excised are an offence to the

Christian belief that none come to God save through Jesus Christ our Lord; and for some it would appear to be a denial of the divinity of Christ.

WHOSE GOD?

73   Who or what is the Great Architect of the Universe (First Degree); the Grand Geometrician (Second Degree); the Most High...the Almighty and Eternal God (Third Degree); the Supreme Being? It has been noted earlier (para. 30) that the evidence of the Grand Lodge to the Working Group introduces a confusion here by speaking in one place of belief in 'a' Supreme Being and in another of belief in 'the' Supreme Being, and revealing the fundamental problem which must face any organisation, secular or ecclesiastical, which attempts to join men of any religion in a single organisation at the heart of which is a common ritual. Given the objective of causing offence to none, it was inevitable that the prayers of the Masonic ritual should involve a Divine Name which would not offend those of non-Christian Faiths: 'The names used for the Supreme Being enable men of different faiths to join in prayer (to God as each sees Him) without the terms of the prayer causing dissension among them. There is no separate Masonic God; a Freemason's God remains the God of the religion he professes' (Leaflet *Freemasonry and Religion* published by the Board for General Purposes). The pamphlet continues: 'Freemasons meet in common respect for the Supreme Being as He remains Supreme for their individual religions, and it is no part of Freemasonry to join religions together...'

74   Before exploring the hazards, real, potential or imagined, of adopting such a view of Freemasonry's ritual activities it needs to be said that Freemasonry has been trying for more than two hundred years to find a solution to a problem not always candidly faced by Christian Churches of the present day when they attempt to organise or participate in "inter-faith" services. How is this to be accomplished without testifying to the pre-eminence of Christ as God's revelation of himself to his world? How is "offence" to members of other faiths to be avoided without minimalising the claims of Christianity? Critical commentators on the quality of Masonic ritual have to examine the extent to which Christian Churches are today themselves prepared to uphold publicly the traditional view that Christianity is not just one religion among many but *the* religion necessary to salvation. The Working Group are well aware of the criticisms that are levelled at Christian Churches' "inter-faith" services.

75   This having been said, Freemasonry itself has no obligation to support the claims of traditional Christianity. It is not and does not claim to be a Christian, even a religious organisation: all it asks is that any and all its members have a belief in 'a' or 'the' Supreme Being. It is up to its members to face the fact that although *they* understand the nature of the God to which prayers are addressed, although *they* may be conscious of addressing *their* God and their Brother addressing *his* in the course of the rituals, the simultaneous worship of the Great Architect at least implies, if it does not actually convey, indifferentism to the claims of distinct religions.

76   The Working Group's evidence contains a number of letters which illustrate the well-known fact that it is possible to have a belief in God (and thus be an acceptable candidate for membership of the Craft) and yet have no personal commitment – to be an "uncommitted Christian". These letters are from men who have subsequently been "converted" to Christ, and have reacted by withdrawing from Freemasonry, finding its rituals inadequate and spiritually damaging. (Cf. Appendix X.)

77   Other letters from both laity and clergy state that in the sometimes many years they have been members of the Craft, they have never felt that there was any incompatibility between their faith and their Freemasonry.

78   It is important to recognise that these contrasting experiences of Freemasonry do exist. Freemasons may understand themselves either to be addressing the God of their own religion or to be addressing the God of different religions under one neutral name. Each position has its own theological problems. Like a good many other organisations, what Freemasonry offers and what its members take from it could depend on factors more personal than the official statements of its aims and objects can either envisage or control.

THE HOLY ROYAL ARCH

79   The focal point of the ceremonies of the Holy Arch is the pedestal, the altar on top of which are spelled out the 'Sacred Words'. The traditional explanation of these words makes Freemasonry most vulnerable to the charge that its prayers and rituals are directed to a syncretistic God.

The Ritual represents the Royal Arch to be the climax of Craft Freemasonry:

> it is intimately blended with all that is nearest and dearest to us in a future state of existence; Divine and human affairs are interwoven so awfully and minutely in all its disquisitions. It has virtue for its aim, the glory of God for its object, and the eternal welfare of man is considered in every part, point and letter of its ineffable mysteries. Suffice it to say, that it is founded on the Sacred Name J...h, who was from all beginning, is now, and will remain one and the same for ever, the Being necessarily existing in and from Himself in all actual perfection, original in His essence.
>
> ......
>
> This Supreme Degree inspires its members with the most exalted ideas of God, leads to the purest and most devout piety, a reverence for the incomprehensible J...h, the eternal Ruler of the Universe, the elemental and primordial source of all its principles, the very spring and fount of all its virtues. (*Mystical Lecture of the Aldersgate Ritual*)

80   How is it then that JAHBULON is frequently thought to be the 'sacred name'; the name of the God on whom the rituals of the Royal Arch are focused? There is no dispute between Freemasons and their fiercest critics that both the word Jehovah and the composite word, Jahbulon, appear on the altar, on top of which is inscribed a circle, containing a triangle. Round the circle is inscribed the name JEHOVAH and on the three sides of the triangle the letters JAH BUL ON. But a dispute there certainly is *in Freemasonry itself*, as to the status and significance to be attached to the two words.

81   The Aldersgate Mystical Lecture states:

> The word on the triangle is that sacred and mysterious name you have just solemnly engaged yourself never to pronounce...It is a compound word, and the combination forms the word...It is in four languages, Chaldee, Hebrew, Syriac, and Egyptian. (J..) is the Chaldee name of God, signifying "His Essence and majesty incomprehensible." It is also a Hebrew word signifying "I am and shall be" thereby expressing the actual, future, and eternal existence of the Most High. (B..) is a Syriac word denoting Lord, or Powerful, it is in itself a compound word, being formed from the preposition B..., in or on, and U., Heaven or on High; therefore the meaning of the word is Lord in Heaven, or on High. (O.) is an Egyptian word signifying Father of All, thereby expressing the Omnipotence of the Father of All, as in that well-known prayer, Our Father, which art in Heaven. The various significations of the words may thus be collected: I am and shall be; Lord in Heaven;

"Father of All! In every age
In every clime adored
By Saint, by savage, and by sage,
Jehovah, Jove or Lord."

82   Just what the average candidate for Exaltation makes of all this is
far beyond the competence of the Working Group to state. What Hannah and other critics of Freemasonry are *quite* clear about is that...

> the secret word is not a Biblical name or a catch-phrase, nor a mumbo-
> jumbo of corrupt Hebrew, but a compound word of quite recognisable ori-
> gin...which claims, together with Jehovah, to be the 'sacred and mysterious
> name of the true and living God most High.' (*Darkness Visible*, p.34)

83   The vigour with which members of the Craft and of the Royal
Arch dispute the matter among themselves can be seen from the
Address to the Grand Chapter of that Degree on 13th November 1985
by Canon Richard Tydeman, reproduced in Appendix IX.

84   Canon Tydeman had raised the matter of the derivation and
interpretation of the word on the triangle six years earlier and with only
a limited success. Now he raised it once again as a matter of some
urgency:

> I am sure that when our ritual was revised in 1936 it all made perfectly good
> sense to those who revised it. Whether it still makes sense today is a matter
> of opinion, for there are so many 'differences' that the situation has become
> absurd. In our Province alone we have twenty-one different Chapters with
> twenty-two different workings!
>
> Has the time come when a new revision is due?...it might be more expedient
> for us to initiate such a revision ourselves, rather than have it forced on us
> by pressure from within and without: for there is no doubt that the con-
> tinued reference to the word on the triangle as *a name* will bring us to disre-
> pute with the world outside, and will cause an increase in the misgiving
> which already exists among our own members.

85   The distinction between the name of God – Jehovah – inscribed
round the circle and the *description* of God – conveyed in the composite
word JAHBULON – inscribed on the side of the triangle is crucial to
Canon Tydeman's argument, as is his own explanation of the derivation of the composite word on the triangle. It is a distinction which
appears to have been originally emphasised in Royal Arch Masonry
but which became less clear as the ritual was promulgated by word of
mouth and local differences inevitably appeared. 'It is, to say the least,
unfortunate that several rituals no longer make this distinction',

observes the United Grand Lodge, 'and that Walton Hannah was able to use one of them as the basis of his damaging comments' (Supplementary evidence of the United Grand Lodge).

86   But even if, as is the case in many other Royal Arch Rituals, the distinction between name and description continues to be stressed and the argument is accepted 'that we can leave Syria and Egypt and Chaldea out of it altogether' and turn to the Hebrew language as the source of 'JAHBULON', the confusion between the status of the words round the circle and on the triangle is not solved since, in Hebrew, description and name are interlocked; the description *is* the 'name'.

87   Nor is this the greatest difficulty to present itself to a Christian and again we come upon a paradox of the rituals of Freemasonry. A Christian already knows the name of God: he does not have to have it revealed to him in a ritual drama. Above all, a Christian is committed to proclaim the name and nature of his God. To have to pretend that the Holy Name is the property of an exclusive, explicitly non-Christian society and to swear on Holy Writ not to reveal it to others is at best absurd and might deservedly be labelled both reprehensible and offensive to Christian conscience.

88   To all this must be added the third and final feature of the top of the pedestal: the Hebrew characters set at the angles of the triangle: Aleph, Beth and Lamed, each of which is said to have reference to the deity or to some divine attribute:

> Take the Aleph and the Beth, they form AB, which is Father; take the Beth, the Aleph, and the Lamed, they form BAL, which is Lord; take the Aleph and the Lamed, they form AL, which means Word; take the Lamed, the Aleph, and the Beth, they form LAB, which signifies Heart or Spirit. Take each combination with the whole, and it will read thus: AB BAL, Father, Lord: AL BAL, Word, Lord; LAB BAL, Spirit, Lord.

The obvious result of such juggling of the Hebrew characters is to emphasise the formation of BAL, the name of a Semitic deity bitterly opposed by Elijah and the later Hebrew prophets; to associate this name in any way with that of Jehovah would have deeply shocked them. It is also a result which gives colour to the view that, in fact, the name on the triangle, far from being a means of describing God, is a syncretistic name for God made out of the name of Yahweh, Baal and Osiris (the Egyptian fertility God).

89   The Supreme Grand Chapter of England of the Royal Arch Degree is as sensible as anyone of the necessity to reconsider the content and implications of its ritual and ceremonies. In advance of the formal report of the meeting of the Grand Chapter held on 12th November 1986, a letter was circulated to Royal Arch Grand Officers and Scribes of the Royal Arch which refers *inter alia* to alterations to the ritual:

> Following recent changes in the Craft Ritual, the President of the Committee of General Purposes gave notice of a resolution for the regular Convocation (of the Grand Chapter) on 11th February 1987 that the physical penalty be removed from the Obligation of the Royal Arch Exaltation ceremony and reference thereto from the Installation Ceremony.

90   The letter also refers to other, highly important, matters relating to the working of the Royal Arch, which were reported by the President of the Committee of General Purposes, who refers to a Working Party who are currently considering

(a) aspects of the Royal Arch Ritual which are known to offend the conscience of Companions and the possibility of shortening the Mystical Lecture

(b) the exchange by the Principals of two words, when their agreement is to keep only one, and

(c) the explanation of the word on the triangle and the characters at the angles of the triangle.

'In due course, Grand Chapter will be asked to consider what changes, if any, should be made.'

91   Just what the proposed changes are, whether the Grand Chapter will accept them, and whether Canon Tydeman's argument is reflected in them, it will be interesting to see. The continued use of ritual which is clearly open to very serious objection from both Masons and non-Masons can only be a grave embarrassment to Freemasonry and a very powerful basis for its critics. First, because Christians reject gnostic claims that further 'revelation' beyond that found in Christ is necessary or possible. Second, the Working Group has concluded that JAHBULON (whether it is a name or description), which appears in all the rituals, must be considered blasphemous: in Christian theology the name of God (Yahweh/Jehovah) must not be taken in vain, nor can it be replaced by an amalgam of the names of pagan deities.

A Peculiar System of Morality?

WORKS OF CHARITY

92   On his introduction into the Craft, the obligation of charity is impressed on every Freemason – 'that virtue which may justly be denominated the distinguishing characteristic of a Freemason's heart':

> In a society so widely extended as Freemasonry, the branches of which are spread over the four quarters of the globe, it cannot be denied that we have many members of rank and opulence; neither can it be concealed that among the thousands who range under its banners, there are some who, from circumstances of unavoidable calamity and misfortune, are reduced to the lowest ebb of poverty and distress. On their behalf it is our usual custom to awaken the feelings of every new-made Brother by such a claim on his charity as his circumstances in life may fairly warrant. (First Degree)

Since at this stage of his initiation the candidate has not only been divested of articles of clothing but of any money he had on his person, it is only possible for him to indicate that, had he money with him, he would willingly have responded to this claim on his charity. When he is in a better position to contribute to the welfare of others he clearly expects and is clearly expected to do so – with the caveat of the Third Degree ritual, 'so far as may be fairly done without detriment to myself or my connections'.

93   Charitable giving has in fact been a feature of Freemasonry from its earliest days, when Masonic Charities were in advance of an unhumanitarian society, and it was this characteristic of its Lodges which explains their exemption from proscription under the Unlawful Societies Act of 1799 and its successor the Seditious Meetings Act of 1817. The earlier Act exempted regular Lodges of Freemasons established before it was passed on the grounds that 'the meetings thereof have been in great manner directed to charitable purposes' (Section 5). Section 36 of the 1817 Act preserved the exemption of Lodges, whether they had held meetings before or after 1799, and also exempted Quakers and any Meeting or Society 'formed or assembled for purposes of a religious or charitable nature only'.

94   Among the earliest beneficiaries of Masonic Charity were first the daughters then the sons of Freemasons who were unable themselves to provide for the education of their children. Later, provision was made for widows and orphans. Later again, attempts were made to provide annuities for 'indigent Brethren' and for their widows. And in 1850 an 'Asylum' was opened for aged Freemasons. Not until 1920 was the Freemasons' Hospital and Nursing Home opened in London – the future of which has been the subject of debate.

95   Whilst it would not be wholly correct to say that Masonic Charity continued exclusively to begin and end "at home", it was still true in 1971 that 'generally speaking Masonic Charity exists, and is generally believed to exist, for Freemasons and their dependants. In this respect Freemasonry differs from such organisations as Rotary and Round Table and others, whose charitable works are not so limited'. (Bagnall Report). It was partly this "inwardness" of Masonic benevolence which caused some anxiety within the Craft and led to the appointment by the Grand Master of the United Lodge of a Committee of Inquiry under the chairmanship of the Hon. Mr Justice Bagnall which was to report not only on the achievements of the charities and their best interest but also on the best interests of the Craft, some of whose members believed that the restrictions of benefit to members prompted unfavourable comparison with other charitable organisations which brought their own into disrepute.

96   The recommendations of the final report, which were accepted by the Grand Master and the Grand Lodge itself, resulted in the establishment of the Grand Charity (1980), whose Council and Petitions Committee deal with the allocations of grants and funds to non-Masonic institutions and organisations. There are now ranges of Masonic charity – Grand Charity, the Masonic Trust for Boys and Girls, and the Foundation for the Aged and Sick. As a matter of policy, the Grand Charity has come to devote roughly a third of its annual expenditure to non-Masonic charities, organisations and institutions, to the great benefit of Universities, the Duke of Edinburgh's Award Scheme, the Girl Guide Association, the National Playing Fields Association, Hospices, the Church of England Children's Society, the St Marylebone Healing and Counselling Centre (Christian Healing Centre) and, each year, a number of cathedrals. In 1984 the contribution to non-Masonic charity was 5 per cent of all *published* Masonic giving.

97   To this centrally administered charitable assistance must be added the assistance of individual Provinces, Districts and Lodges, in time as well as money, to local non-Masonic as well as Masonic needs.

98   There can be no doubt that Freemasonry is justly proud of the extent of its charitable giving. In a world where human need is a major problem, contributions to alleviate need and suffering must be welcomed and harnessed. However, charitable giving is not to be equated with Christianity. The Christian faith sees its charitable giving as a response to the love of God in Christ (not just a response to human need) and as an integral part of the mission of God in the world. "Buying your way into Heaven" is impossible.

RIGHT CONDUCT

99   Benevolence and Charity are the first Masonic virtues to which an Entered Apprentice is introduced on his Initiation. In the Charge which follows Initiation, the 'solid foundation on which Freemasonry rests – the practice of every moral and social virtue' is spelled out at length:

> As a Freemason, let me recommend to your most serious contemplation the V(olume) of S(acred) L(aw), charging you to consider it as the unerring standard of truth and justice and to regulate your actions by the divine precepts it contains. Therein you will be taught the important duties you owe to God, to your neighbour and to yourself...

> As a citizen of the world, I am to enjoin you to be exemplary in the discharge of your civil duties...

> As an individual, let me recommend the practice of every domestic duty as well as public virtue; let Prudence direct you, Temperance chasten you, Fortitude support you, and Justice be the guide of all your actions...

> And as a last general recommendation, let me exhort you to dedicate yourself to such pursuits as may at once enable you to be respectable in life, useful to mankind, and an ornament to the society of which you have this day become a member...

100   In all Lodges under the jurisdiction of the United Grand Lodge, the Bible lies open and it is this V S L to which the mind of the Christian Freemason is drawn. Yet the Bible is immeasurably more than a guide to good and proper moral conduct. It is the record of God's revelation of himself to man and his incarnation in human form to achieve the redemption of man from sin by his own self-offering on the Cross. The

First Degree lecture, however, speaks of attaining the 'Ethereal Mansion' through the exercise of Faith, Hope and Charity.

In the Ritual of the Second Degree, the candidate is instructed:

> But as we are not all operative Masons, but rather free and accepted, or speculative, we apply these *ts* [tools] to our morals. In this sense, the Sq [Square] teaches morality, the L [Level] equality, and the PR [Plumb Rule] justness and uprightness of life and actions. Thus by square conduct, level steps, and upright intentions we hope to ascend to those immortal mansions whence all goodness emanates.

At the conclusion in the ceremony of Raising, or the ritual of the Third of the Craft Degrees, the newly 'raised' Master Mason is told:

> Thus the working tools of a Master Mason teach us to bear in mind, and act according to, the laws of our Divine Creator, that, when we shall be summoned from this sublunary abode, we may ascend to the Grand Lodge above, where the world's Great Architect lives and reigns for ever.

The question arises: Is the Master Mason being assured that if he lives a good and moral life he will inevitably 'ascend' to live with his Creator? Is this really what is meant? Comforting though it may be for some, it appears to have the marks of a familiar English heresy – Pelagianism – since the grace and forgiveness of God in Christ and the power of the Holy Spirit are being ignored. The Working Group cannot therefore accept the statement in the United Grand Lodge's leaflet (referred to in paras. 58 and 73) that Freemasonry 'does not claim to lead to salvation by works, by secret knowledge, or by any other means'. It seems to the Working Group that, in the light of the extracts quoted above, salvation by works is both implicit and explicit in the rituals.

Comments and Questions

101 Throughout their work, the Group appreciated that they were expected to produce a document which could form the basis of a fair and informed debate in the General Synod on a particular aspect of Freemasonry in this country. The Group itself was appointed with that in mind. Two who were deliberately included were Freemasons themselves, but the remaining five were equally deliberately chosen not as either "for" or "against" the Craft but as representing a range of churchmanship and skills.

102 Since inclusion of Freemasons has been criticised by some who wrote to the Group's Secretary it is worth emphasising that, far from it being intended that this should weight the Group's final paper, it was a conscious attempt to ensure that it was not open to the immediate objection that "not one of them knew what they were talking about" – a stricture very commonly made by Freemasons on the comments of non-Masons on the Craft and most recently on the Methodist Report considered by the Methodist Conference in 1985.

103 The Group were also sensible of the fact that there are many members of the Church of England who are practising Freemasons and see no conflict between their membership of the two bodies. A few of them are so uncritical of Freemasonry as to write protesting against the decision of the General Synod even to embark on the present exercise. On the other hand, it is simply foolish to ignore both the fact that there is currently a wave of anxiety among Christians of different dominations regarding the very question to which the Group have directed their attention, and the fact that the Group itself has received evidence confirming what was already generally known – that some Christians, themselves once Freemasons, have left the Craft precisely because they perceived their membership of it as being in conflict with their Christian witness and belief.

104 From the evidence we have received it is clear that some Christians have found the impact of Masonic rituals disturbing and a few perceive them as positively evil. The dramatic impact of the rituals has had a "psychic" effect (cf. Appendix X).

105 The evidence the Group has received, however, points to the fact that there is, and has been for many years, an element of self-criticism among Freemasons themselves which, largely due to an inbuilt and somewhat excessive disposition to "privacy" about their organisation, has not been given very wide publicity.

106 As has already been noted, such secrecy as the Craft may have originally aspired to was historically short-lived (cf. para. 22) and is in the present day virtually non-existent. Freemasons themselves prefer to use the word privacy and regard themselves as best described as a private society. Nevertheless, every one of the Craft Rituals and the Rituals of the Holy Royal Arch on the Admission, Passing, Raising or Installation refers time and again to 'secrets'; 'secrets' which the candidate pledges himself never to reveal or 'unduly obtain' *(Emulation Ritual,* p.103); 'secrets' the full nature of which is not disclosed until after the candidate has pledged himself to silence by either placing his hand on or kissing the Bible or the Sacred Book of his Faith.

107 It is abundantly clear that many accept this procedure merely as a necessary requirement of membership of a society which they are anxious to join and whose fellowship they look forward to enjoying. Some will attach little importance to the query which has often been raised (cf. para. 56) but the question surely remains: Is it acceptable for a Christian to swear by solemn oath never to reveal 'secrets' the full nature of which is not disclosed to him until after he has pledged himself to lifelong silence – even though he will have been assured in advance that he will be asked to undertake 'nothing incompatible with your civil, moral, or religious duties'? *(Emulation Ritual,* p.74).

108 There also remains the additional question inherent in the teaching of Masonic ritual and the use to which it is to be put: the development of moral habits of mind and conduct of such kind as to benefit not only the community but the man himself by so moulding his character as to enable him to triumph over death and 'ascend to those immortal mansions whence all goodness emanates' *(Emulation Ritual,* p.139).

109 What Masonic rituals clearly imply is that Freemasonry is a way to live and die and the way to be in a right relationship with God. Since the virtues of Faith, Hope and Charity are acknowledged Christian virtues, how can Christians take exception to an organisation which very strongly urges their practice? Critics dwell on the absence of any refer-

ence to the uniqueness of the death and of the resurrection of Christ which alone secure our "right relationship with God" and the indwelling power of the Holy Spirit. On the other hand, modern Masonry has never pretended to be a Christian organisation; nor, so far as can be deduced from its rituals, does it make any comment on the teaching of Christianity or any religion other than to assert that its secrets are not incompatible with an individual's religious duties. The very basis of the claim that Freemasonry is a 'support' of religion, not a religion itself, is the fact that it is open to members of any religion, and is concerned with spiritual values and right conduct, which it conveys and instills in its members by the ritual dramas at the meetings of the Lodge, during which discussion and debate of religion are excluded as a matter of policy. Nevertheless, with no reference to the grace of God in Jesus Christ, the charge remains that the teaching of the ritual is Pelagian (see para. 100).

110   The Working Group are at one in rejecting the assertion that the rituals of the Craft contain no element of worship (cf. para. 68). As would be expected, there was considerable discussion and diversity of view on the implications of the qualification for its membership and the character of its rituals. Historically, Craft Masonry represents typical eighteenth-century Deism. Must this be taken, in the later twentieth century, to represent a slur or slight on Christianity? The conviction, echoed in the Group itself, that this is indeed the case was expressed with some force in submissions to the Working Group:

> If the unique claims of Christianity are to be taken seriously how can a man claiming to be a Christian belong to a Deist organisation in which there is a free and easy acceptance of any religion – Hindu, Sikh, Muslim, Jew *et al.* – whose God(s) are their own and wholly alien to the God of the New Testament?

> Has the Christian not a clear duty and an overwhelming responsibility continually to witness to the higher claims of Christianity?

111   Such arguments form a conspicuous part of the reasoning behind the continued prohibition on membership of Freemasonry placed by the Roman Catholic Church on its adherents.

112   These questions need to be considered in the context of contemporary interest in and experiment with inter-faith services. Only last year, the Bishop of Rome himself was in Assisi praying for peace alongside Buddhists, Sikhs, Jews, and medicine men of North Ameri-

can Indian tribes. When he listened attentively to their prayers was he joining in them or unobtrusively dissociating himself from what was going on? Was the whole affair, in which the Archbishop of Canterbury was himself prominent, just an exhibition of spiritual sleight-of-hand or ecclesiastical hypocrisy?

113   In the course of the Working Group's discussion, the question was raised as to whether there is a critical difference between "one-off" or occasional inter-faith services and the rituals regularly associated with the formal meetings of a Lodge. The Group came to the view that in either case theological indifferentism was a distinct possibility and, some would say, even a probability.

114   Among the evidence received by the Group were letters from Freemasons, indicating an alternative view of the consequences of Lodge meetings; that the social relationships established by meeting in Lodge actually made it possible outside its formal business to discuss and explain the peculiar claims of Christianity over any other religion. One (clerical) Freemason in fact referred to bringing men to be confirmed in the Church of England as a result of meeting them as members of his Lodge.

115   Members of General Synod will need to take such testimony into account when they consider the effects of Freemasonry on its present and past members, just as they will have to reflect on the evidence referred to in paras. 104 and 105.

116   They will also have to give careful consideration to two other, not unrelated, criticisms of the Craft. First, that if Freemasonry knows of a way of establishing a right relationship with God, then it has a moral obligation to share this knowledge with all others. Second, that if it can reveal, in the ritual of the Holy Royal Arch, the true name of God, then it should certainly not conceal this name from others. The God and Father of our Lord Jesus Christ is not the property of an exclusive, all-male organisation; he is revealed for all.

117   With regard to the first criticism, it has to be recognised that the Craft claims to a peculiar but not exclusive knowledge. This however does not really answer the objection that whatever knowledge it has which might help in our earthly pilgrimage, it should, by Christian standards, be willingly shared with all.

118 More important – some members of the Working Group would judge far more important – is the criticism brought against the Holy Royal Arch not merely relating to the vexed problem of words and letters inscribed on the top of the altar but regarding the requirements of members of Holy Royal Arch Chapters that the name of God revealed in the course of the ritual is in no circumstances to be revealed to or even pronounced in the company of those not members of a Chapter.

119 The Working Group recognise the present concern of Grand Chapter to re-interpret the composite word on the triangle. Nevertheless it does not seem at all likely or indeed possible that attempts at re-interpretation can possibly meet the fundamental objection to the Ritual of the Holy Royal Arch; that it professes to reveal the 'true name of God', a name which, on their most solemn oath, members are pledged not to disclose to others. How can such a pledge be honoured by Christians?

120 Members of General Synod, among whom there will almost certainly be other members of the Craft in addition to the two who are members of the present Working Group, will be advised to read and reflect upon recently published histories of the emergence of the United Grand Lodge. They will find that the inclusion of the Holy Royal Arch as an element of modern Craft Masonry was a matter of dispute in the early nineteenth century and they may wonder whether its acceptance has altogether added to the credibility of Craft Masonry in the late twentieth century.

121 Compared with such fundamental matters, the much publicised issue of the nature of what are now known officially as the 'traditional' oaths, seems less important. The Working Group were advised from the outset that the United Grand Lodge was proposing to withdraw them from the rituals over which it had control and later that the Grand Chapter of the Holy Royal Arch was proposing to make similar modifications in its own ritual (which both have recently done). As has already been noted (cf. para. 52) they are still referred to in detail elsewhere in the rituals of the three Craft Degrees.

FACING THE QUESTION THE GENERAL SYNOD POSED

122   This Report has identified a number of important issues on which, in the view of the Working Group, the General Synod will have to reflect as it considers 'the compatibility or otherwise of Freemasonry with Christianity'. The reflections of the Working Group itself reveal understandable differences of opinion between those who are Freemasons and those who are not. Whilst the former fully agree that the Report shows that there are clear difficulties to be faced by Christians who are Freemasons, the latter are of the mind that the Report points to a number of very fundamental reasons to question the compatibility of Freemasonry with Christianity.

On behalf of the Working Group

May 1987   MARGARET HEWITT
                                        Chairman

Appendix I

See para. 13

For example Stephen Knight's book – *The Brotherhood: the Secret World of the Freemasons* (1984) — is vulnerable to the criticism that it was ill researched and included unconfirmed data. The United Grand Lodge, in its evidence, referred to the following 'factual inaccuracies' in the book:

(a) James Page, discredited Commissioner of the City of London Police, could not have owed his various promotions to his having been a Freemason as he did not join the Craft until after he became Commissioner;

(b) Knight's claim that the Lord Chancellor's patronage office was staffed by Freemasons was publicly denied by Lord Hailsham in letters to The Times, The Telegraph and The Guardian;

(c) At the time the book was published, none of the permanent Officers of the government of the City of London were Freemasons. Many of the persons Knight categorically states to have been present at the meeting of Guildhall Lodge which he describes were absent from the meeting;

(d) Knight's claim that the Registers of English Lodges in the Far East were kept tightly secret for the period during which Sir Roger Hollis was in residence is nonsense. Sir Roger was in any case not a Mason.

Appendix II

THE CHRISTIAN DEGREES

See para. 15

This Report does not attempt any detailed examination of rituals of other than those of the three Craft Degrees and of the Holy Royal Arch. There are also, however, the 'Christian Degrees': the Rose Croix, the Knights Templar, the Knights of Malta, and the Red Cross of Constantine.

All but the Rose Croix explicitly require prior membership of the Holy Royal Arch. It becomes of special importance, therefore, that attention is paid to the implications for Christians of membership of the Holy Royal Arch.

Admission to the Rose Croix, which is governed by the Supreme Council of the 33rd Degree (cf. Appendix VI), requires prior membership of the seventeen Degrees of the Antient and Accepted Rite of Freemasonry. The Degrees of Craft Masonry, which each candidate must already have received, are accepted as equivalent to the first three Degrees of this Rite. The next fourteen are awarded in name only in England as a preface to initiation into the Rose Croix – the eighteenth degree of the 'Higher Degrees' (cf. para 39). The selected candidate is required to profess the Trinitarian and Christian Faith and be willing to take an Obligation in the Name of the Holy and Undivided Trinity.

Appendix III

WOMEN'S FREEMASONRY

All the information in this Report relates to *men's* Lodges of the Craft. There *are* women Freemasons, but they are under the jurisdiction of the Grand Lodge of the Honourable Fraternity of Ancient Freemasons, an exclusively female movement which emerged in 1913.

The 42/44 Lodges of the women's Fraternity are in almost every respect a mirror image of their male counterparts. They observe the same protocol, set out in the four hundred pages of the Supreme Grand Chapter Regulations; they progress through the ranks in the same way as do the men. According to a recent article 'They take pride in emulating the men exactly' (*New Society*, 18 Oct. 1985, p.94). Nevertheless, their Lodges are not recognised by the United Grand Lodge. Indeed, the fourth of the 'Basic Principles for Grand Lodge Recognition' specifically states:

> That membership of the Grand Lodge and individual Lodges shall be exclusively of men: and that each Grand Lodge shall have no Masonic intercourse of any kind with mixed Lodges or bodies which admit women to membership. (*Information for the Guidance of Members of the Craft*, 1985, p.3)

However, would-be members of the Fraternity (according to an article in *The Times*, 17 June 1985) must get their husband's agreement before they are considered for membership. If this is correct, since many who belong to the Honourable Fraternity are those whose husbands are Freemasons too, a degree of acceptance, if not approval, must exist.

As regards the "mixed" Lodges, there is at present no information to hand but according to the *New Society* article the Honourable Fraternity itself 'grew from the co-masons, a mixed off-shoot of the men's movement...[and] rapidly became single sex'.

Appendix IV

GRAND LODGES IN EUROPE RECOGNISED AS REGULAR BY THE UNITED GRAND LODGE OF ENGLAND:

Grand Lodge of Austria	Grand Orient of Italy
Regular Grand Lodge of Belgium	Grand Lodge of Luxembourg

National Grand Lodge of Denmark†	Grand East of the Netherlands
Grand Lodge of Finland†	Grand Lodge of Norway†
Grande Loge Nationale Française	Grand Lodge of Scotland
Grand Lodge of Ireland*	Grand Lodge of Sweden† [Sweden only]
United Grand Lodges of Germany	Grand Lodge Alpina of
Grand Lodge of Greece	Switzerland
National Grand Lodge of Iceland	Grand Lodge of Turkey

† for Christians
* includes the Republic of Ireland and Northern Ireland

Appendix V

(Reproduced from the evidence submitted by the United Grand Lodge)
AIMS AND RELATIONSHIPS OF THE CRAFT

On 5 August 1920, at the direction of the Grand Master, the Grand Secretary wrote as fol-lows to the Editor of the Daily Telegraph:

Sir,
    As a great deal of misapprehension appears to be entertained in some quarters concerning the aims and relationships of the United Grand Lodge of Antient, Free and Accepted Masons of England, I have been desired by the Grand Master to make the following statement regarding them.

The Grand Lodge of England – of which H.R.H. The Duke of Connaught has been for twenty years Grand Master, in succession to the late King Edward VII, himself Grand Master as Prince of Wales, from 1875 to 1901 – has held strictly aloof throughout its history, which dates from 1717, from participation in public or political affairs, either national or international, considering itself precluded from taking any share in discussions on state policy. While thus standing aside from party divisions it has always inculcated patriotism in the citizen, and loyalty in the individual. It had not long been establised when it publicly gave assurance of this to one of His Majesty's Principal Secretaries of State. The assurance thus given in the reign of George I is emphasized in a spe-cial degree in that of George V. Everyone who comes into Freemasonry is strictly enjoined at the outset not to countenance any act which may have a tendency to subvert the peace and good order of society, to pay a due obedi-ence to the law of any State in which he resides, and never to be remiss in the allegiance due to his Sovereign.

No secret is attaching to these duties, which are of the essence of Masonry as practised under the Jurisdiction of the United Grand Lodge of England, as well as by the Sister Grand Lodges of Ireland, Scotland, Canada, Australia and New Zealand, and, I have reason to believe, of the remainder of the English-speaking world.

Every English Lodge at its consecration is dedicated to God and to His Service; no one can become a Mason until he has declared his faith in the Supreme Being. As a consequence, men of every shade of political opinion and ministers of all religious denominations are members of and office-bearers in our organization, and Masonry thus provides a platform on which men of all conditions, classes, and creeds can work together for the common welfare. In Masonic Lodges all discussions on topics of a political or theological nature are strictly forbidden.

Because of its determination to preserve the position it has upheld for over two centuries, the Grand Lodge of England never takes part in any Masonic or quasi-Masonic gathering in which the fundamental Antient Landmarks of Freemasonry – which have been indicated above – are allowed to be regarded as open questions.

Yours faithfully,

P. COLVILLE SMITH,

Grand Secretary.

The letter was published on 7 August 1920 (with editorial comment), and reported to Grand Lodge at its next quarterly communication on 1 September 1920.

In August, 1938, the Grand Lodges of England, Ireland and Scotland each agreed upon and issued a statement identical in terms except that the name of the issuing Grand Lodge appeared throughout. This statement was in the following terms:-

AIMS AND RELATIONSHIPS OF THE CRAFT

1. From time to time the United Grand Lodge of England has deemed it desirable to set forth in precise form the aims of Freemasonry as consistently practised under its Jurisdiction since it came into being as an organised body in 1717, and also to define the principles governing its relations with those other Grand Lodges with which it is in fraternal accord.

2. In view of representations which have been received, and of statements recently issued which have distorted or obscured the true objects of Freemasonry, it is once again considered necessary to emphasize certain fundamental principles of the Order.

3. The first condition of admission into, and membership of, the Order is a belief in the Supreme Being. This is essential and admits of no compromise.

4. The Bible, referred to by Freemasons as the Volume of the Sacred Law, Law, is always open in the Lodges. Every candidate is required to take his Obligation on that book or on the Volume which is held by his particular creed to impart sanctity to an oath or promise taken upon it.

5. Everyone who enters Freemasonry is, at the outset, strictly forbidden to countenance any act which may have a tendency to subvert the peace and good order of society; he must pay due obedience to the law of any State in which he resides or which may afford him protection, and he must never be remiss in the allegiance due to the Sovereign of his native land.

6. While English Freemasonry thus inculcates in each of its members the duties of loyalty and citizenship, it reserves to the individual the right to hold his own opinion with regard to public affairs. But neither in any Lodge, nor at any time in his capacity as a Freemason, is he permitted to discuss or to advance his views on theological or political questions.

7. The Grand Lodge has always consistently refused to express any opinion on questions of foreign or domestic State policy either at home or abroad, and it will not allow its name to be associated with any action, however humanitarian it may appear to be, which infringes its unalterable policy of standing aloof from every question affecting the relations between one government and another, or between political parties, or questions as to rival theories of government.

8. The Grand Lodge is aware that there do exist Bodies, styling themselves Freemasons, which do not adhere to these principles, and while that attitude exists the Grand Lodge of England refuses absolutely to have any relations with such Bodies, or to regard them as Freemasons.

9. The Grand Lodge of England is a Sovereign and independent Body practising Freemasonry only within the three Degrees and only within the limits defined in its Constitutions as "pure Antient Masonry." It does not recognise or admit the existence of any superior Masonic authority, however styled.

10. On more than one occasion the Grand Lodge has refused, and will continue to refuse, to participate in conferences with so-called International Associations claiming to represent Freemasonry, which admit to membership Bodies failing to conform strictly to the principles upon which the Grand Lodge of England is founded. The Grand Lodge does not admit any such claim, nor can its views be represented by any such Association.

11. There is no secret with regard to any of the basic principles of Freemasonry, some of which have been stated above. The Grand Lodge will always consider the recognition of those Grand Lodges which profess, and practise, and can show that they have consistently professed and practised those established and unaltered principles, but in no circumstances will it enter into discussion with a view to any new or varied interpretation of them. They must be accepted and practised wholeheartedly and in their entirety by those who desire to be recognised as Freemasons by the United Grand Lodge of England.

This statement was reported in the Daily Telegraph on 29 August 1938 (and was the subject of editorial comment). It was reported to Grand Lodge at its next quarterly communication on 7 September 1938. It was ordered to be read in every Lodge, and a copy was ordered to be given to every Mason of the English Constitution. Attention was again drawn to the statement at the quarterly communication of Grand Lodge on 7 June 1944.

At the quarterly communicaton on 7 September 1949, Grand Lodge approved the following addition to the declaration of 1938.

The Grand Lodge of England has been asked if it still stands by this declaration, particularly in regard to paragraph 7. The Grand Lodge of England replied that it stood by every word of the declaration, and has since asked for the opinion of the Grand Lodges of Ireland and Scotland. A conference has been held between the three Grand Lodges, and all unhesitatingly reaffirm the statement that was pronounced in 1938: nothing in present-day affairs has been found that could cause them to recede from that attitude.

If Freemasonry once deviated from its course by expressing an opinion on political or theological questions, it would be called upon not only publicly to approve or denounce any movement which might arise in the future, but would sow the seeds of discord among its own members.

The three Grand Lodges are convinced that it is only by this rigid adherence to this policy that Freemasonry has survived the constantly changing doctrines of the outside world, and are compelled to place on record their complete disapproval of any action which may tend to permit the slightest departure from the basic principles of Freemasonry. They are strongly of opinion that if any of the three Grand Lodges does so, it cannot maintain a claim to be following the Antient Landmarks of the Order, and must ultimately face disintegration.

Appendix VI

THE FURTHER DEGREES OF FREEMASONRY

The Craft Degrees

(1) Entered Apprentice
(2) Fellow Craft
(3) Master Mason

The Further Degrees

(4) Secret Master
(5) Perfect Master
(6) Intimate Secretary
(7) Provost and Judge
(8) Intendant of the Buildings

(9)   Elect of Nine
(10)   Elect of Fifteen
(11)   Sublime Elect
(12)   Grand Master Architect
(13)   Royal Arch of Enoch
(14)   Grand Elect Perfect and Sublime Master
(15)   Knight of the Sword or of the East
(16)   Prince of Jerusalem
(17)   Knight of the East and West
(18)   Knight of the Pelican and Eagle, the Sovereign Prince Rose Croix of Heredom
(19)   Grand Pontiff
(20)   Venerable Grand Master
(21)   Patriarch Noachite
(22)   Prince of Libanus
(23)   Chief of the Tabernacle
(24)   Prince of the Tabernacle
(25)   Knight of the Brazen Serpent
(26)   Prince of Mercy
(27)   Commander of the Temple
(28)   Knight of the Sun
(29)   Knight of St Andrew
(30)   Grand Elected Knight Kadosh, Knight of the Black and White Eagle
(31)   Grand Inspector Inquisitor Commander
(32)   Sublime Prince of the Royal Secret
(33)   Grand Inspector General

Appendix VII

UNITED GRAND LODGE OF ENGLAND
FREEMASONS' HALL
GREAT QUEEN STREET
LONDON WC2B 5AZ

June 1986

Dear Sir and Brother,

PENALTIES IN THE OBLIGATIONS

On 11 June, Grand Lodge approved by a large majority the Resolution to omit all references to physical penalties from the Obligation in the three Degrees and in the Installation, but to retain them elsewhere in the ceremonies.

The recommended alterations to the ritual, which were also approved by Grand Lodge in June, were set out in the Appendix to the Report of the Board of General Purposes to Grand Lodge.

I enclose a copy of the recommended alterations, which have been expanded to avoid any ambiguity.

The Board sees it as important that the Resolution is put into effect as soon as possible, particularly in so far as it affects Initiations. In any event, the changes should be implemented not later than June 1987.

Yours faithfully and fraternally,

M.B.S. HIGHAM

Grand Secretary.

Enc: Recommended alterations

Distribution:

For action
Provincial Grand Masters
District Grand Masters
Grand Inspectors
Secretaries of Lodges directly administered from Freemasons' Hall

For information
Grand Officers

THE PENALTIES – RECOMMENDED ALTERATIONS

FIRST DEGREE

OBLIGATION – Physical penalty omitted, moral penalty left in, giving wording as:

> ...these several points I solemnly swear to observe, without evasion, equivocation, or mental reservation of any kind, in the certain knowledge that on the violation of any of them I shall be branded as a wilfully perjured ... etc.

THE THREE GREAT DANGERS – This passage has to be re-worded and an addition made as:

> Bro..., by your meek and candid behaviour this evening, you have, symbolically, escaped two great dangers, but there was a third which, traditionally, would have awaited you until the latest period of your existence. The dangers you have escaped are those of s and s, for on your entrance into the

Lodge this p was presented to your n l b to imply that, had you rashly attempted to rush forward, you would have been accessory to your own death by s, whilst the brother who held it would have remained firm and done his duty; there was likewise this c t with a running n about your n which would have rendered any attempt at retreat equally fatal. But the danger which, traditionally, would have awaited you until your latest hour was the physical penalty at one time associated with the Obligation of a mason had you improperly disclosed the secrets of masonry, that of having t t c a, t t t o b t r and b i t s o t s at l w m or a c's l f t s, where t t r e a f t i 24 hrs. The inclusion of such a penalty is unnecessary, for the Obligation you have taken this evening is binding upon you for so long as you shall live.

ENTRUSTMENT – WM illustrates sn., Can. copies. WM explains that it alludes:

...to the symbolic penalty of the degree, which implied that, as a man of honour, a mason would rather have had his t c a than improperly disclose ... etc.

EXCHANGE WITH SENIOR WARDEN – When SW asks, to what does it allude? answer:

...the symbolic penalty of the degree, which implied that, as a man of honour, a mason would rather have had his t c a than improperly disclose ... etc.

SECOND DEGREE

PLEDGE AFTER QUESTIONS AND BEFORE ENTRUSTMENT WITH PW – change to:

Do you likewise pledge yourself that you will conceal what I shall now impart to you with the same strict caution as the other secrets in masonry?

OBLIGATION – Penalty omitted, giving wording as:

...I solemnly swear to observe, without evasion, equivocation or mental reservation of any kind. So help me ... etc.

ENTRUSTMENT – WM illustrates p sn., Can. copies. WM explains that it alludes:

...to the symbolic penalty at one time included in the Obligation in this degree had he improperly disclosed the secrets entrusted to him, which implied that, as a man of honour, a FCFM would rather have had the l b l o, t h t t and g t t r bs of t a or d bts o t f a p.

EXCHANGE WITH SENIOR WARDEN – When SW asks, to what does it allude? answer:

The symbolic penalty of this degree, which implied that, as a man of honour, a FCFM would rather have had his h t f h b than improperly disclose...etc.

49

THIRD DEGREE

PLEDGE AFTER QUESTIONS AND BEFORE ENTRUSTMENT WITH PW – change to:

> Do you likewise pledge yourself that you will conceal what I shall now impart to you with the same strict caution as the other secrets in masonry?

OBLIGATION – Penalty omitted, giving wording as:

> ...I solemnly swear to observe, without evasion, equivocation or mental reservation of any kind. So help me...etc.

ENTRUSTMENT – WM explains p sn., Can. copies. WM explains that it alludes:

> ...to the symbolic penalty at one time included in the Obligation in this degree had he improperly disclosed the secrets entrusted to him, which implied that, as a man of honour, a MM would rather have been s i t, the b b t a and t a s over t f o e and w b t f e w o h, that no trace or remembrance of so vile a wretch may longer be found among men, particularly MMs.

INSTALLATION

OBLIGATION – Penalty omitted, giving wording as:

> ...I solemnly swear to observe, without evasion, equivocation or mental reservation of any kind. So help me...etc.

AFTER SEALING OF OBLIGATION – with ME still in the same position IM says to ME:

> The symbolic penalty which a Master-elect was formerly called on to repeat in his Obligation was that of...etc.

and IM continues with reference to the three Great Lights.
(If it is felt that the ME's hands should be removed from the VSL while the explanation of the penalty is given, this may be done.)

Appendix VIII

Reproduced from the United Grand Lodge's letter of 11 June 1986 to Grand Officers and to Secretaries of Lodges

Appendix C

THE PENALTIES IN THE OBLIGATIONS
Report by Board of General Purposes

Following the request of the MW The Grand Master, the Board has been considering the penalties in the Obligations, and is convinced that, while preserving the familiar and time-honoured wording, it would be in the interests of the Craft that they should be removed from the Obligations altogether, and included in some other part of the Ritual. Notice of Motion was given by the President at the Quarterly Communication in March 1986, and the Resolution appears as item 5(i) of the Paper of Business.

The MW the Grand Master first voiced his misgivings about the physical penalties as long as ago as 1979, when he said, whilst addressing the Grand Lodge at the Annual Investiture on 25th April:

> "I remember feeling a very definite sensation of repugnance when I came to repeat the penalties clause in its old form"…and went on to refer to "the distasteful aspect of calling upon God to witness an Oath which is scarcely practical and certainly barbarous"…

He again referred to the matter when presiding at the Quarterly Communication of the Grand Lodge on 13th March, 1985, when he said:

> "It seems to me that it would not be a very radical step, and would in no way affect the meaning of the Ritual, if the penalties were removed entirely from the Obligations, and treated as a form of traditional history."

A previous discussion of this matter was initiated by the late Bishop Herbert in 1964, and at the Quarterly Communication of the Grand Lodge in December of that year the so-called permissive variations were approved. They were, as many feel, an unsatisfactory compromise, and have only gained partial acceptance by Lodges; the same moral question, however, remains.

Before his obligation, a Candidate is told that vows of fidelity are required, but that in those vows there is nothing incompatible with his civil, moral or religious duties. A solemn oath is then taken by him on the Volume of the Sacred Law, and the help of God is invoked. But embedded in the Obligation are the physical penalties, to enforce which would involve a serious criminal offence, and which comes as a surprise and a shock to the Candidate so soon after he has been assured that there is nothing in them incompatible with his civil, moral or religious duties. In the days of 250 years ago, when the law provided for the penalty of death by hanging for quite a number of what we should today consider minor offences, it might have been just acceptable to put a gruesome penalty into such an Obligation, but in the present day the law and circumstances have both changed to an extent when such penalties are offensive and unacceptable. In such a serious matter as an Obligation it must be considered whether the penalties included are really meant or not. Clearly they cannot be, and never could have been, actually enforced, even 250 years ago. If therefore the penalties in the Obligations are not really meant, this must throw doubt on whether the Obligation is binding so far as the other, more important, matters it contains are concerned. If the penalty part of the Obligation has no force because it could not be carried out, then it can be removed, not just without detriment to the solemnity of the oath, but in fact with a strengthening of the remaining points. The oath or Obligation does not require a physical penalty to make it binding; it stands in its own right being taken in the presence of the Great Architect of the Universe. Standing where they do in the Obligation, the physical penalties often come as a surprise to candidates, however well they have been prepared, and the shock involved in hearing them in this way has deterred many from continuing to progress in masonry. The existence of the physical penalties also gives ready material for attack by our enemies and detractors.

For these reasons the Board unanimously recommends the Grand Lodge to approve the Resolution.

The Board also wishes to make the following points:

(a) Physical penalties in their present position in the Obligations are not a landmark of the Order. Although known in other connections, they seem to have been introduced in the present position from about 1730.

(b) Grand Lodge has undoubted power to give directions on matters of Ritual, and has done so on several occasions in the past.

(c) The Resolution deals with a matter of principle and not of detail. The Board believes that the manner in which any alterations are made should involve as little change as possible, be reasonably consistent throughout the whole of the English Constitution, and retain, wherever possible, the accepted wording that Lodges and Ritual workings have used for so long.

N.B. After debate on 11 June 1986 Grand Lodge resolved that "all references to physical penalties be omitted from the Obligations taken by Candidates in the three Degrees and by a Master Elect at his Installation but retained elsewhere in the respective ceremonies".

Appendix IX

CANON TYDEMAN'S ADDRESS

Reproduced from the United Grand Lodge's letter of 11 December 1985 to Grand Officers and to Secretaries of Lodges.

THE WORDS ON THE TRIANGLE – AN ALTERNATIVE VIEW

An address to Grand Chapter on 13 November 1985 by E Comp the Revd Canon Richard Tydeman, Grand Superintendent in and over Suffolk.

ME Pro First Grand Principal and Companions, recent attacks on Freemasonry have shown up all too clearly that the Royal Arch is one of our most vulnerable fronts, and the thing that our critics have seized upon as proof of our evil intentions is the composite word or words on the triangle in the very centre of every Chapter.

Unfortunately we are not giving the right impression at all. Only the other day I was accosted by a vociferous churchwarden: "How can you", he said, "How can you, a minister of religion, take part in ceremonies which invoke heathen gods by name?", and as evidence for his accusations, he brandished before me, me, not a copy of Stephen Knight's book, but a copy of the minutes of last November's Grand Chapter containing the address by ME Comp the Revd Francis Heydon, the then Third Grand Principal.

Let me say at once that I have no wish to quarrel with E Comp Heydon, who is a personal friend of mine, and I know he based his talk on an article by the late E Comp Norman Hackney for whom I had a great respect. All the same, I am afraid I must beg to differ from their conclusions.

Let me remind you of what was said last year: that the words on the triangle are intended as a description of God "as the three original Grand Masters might have done so, remembering that they all spoke different languages", the three languages quoted being Hebrew, Syriac, and Egyptian. Norman Hackney, in his original article went even further than that and maintained that here we have "the *Name* of God in three languages; just that: no more and no less."

Now, Companions, in my view this explanation falls to the ground because it is based on the false assumption that Hiram Abiff was (let me quote again from last year) "a Kenite of the tribes that lived on the shores of the Red Sea in part of the Egyptian empire", and would have spoken Egyptian. Where this idea came from I cannot imagine, because Scripture informs us quite clearly in two places, that Hiram Abiff's mother was a widow, of one of the northernmost tribes of Israel, as far from Egypt as you could get, and his late father had been a man of Tyre, which was even further away, so although Hiram could have spoken both Hebrew and Syriac, he certainly would not have addressed God in Egyptian.

The absurdity of the situation can be illustrated by a modern parallel: it would be like saying that a man whose mother came from Newcastle-upon-Tyne and father from Edinburgh is therefore likely to speak with a cockney accent.

Tradition dies hard and it may well be that many zealous companions will go on quoting Syriac and Egyptian and perpetuating this extraordinary jumble of explanations. I will not say that they are *wrong* but I will say that I think they are definitely unwise in the present climate of opinion. As the Apostle Paul once remarked: "All things are lawful unto me, but all things are not expedient" – and it is most certainly not expedient to lay ourselves open to charges of idolatry or syncretism at a time when Churches are seriously examining our beliefs and doctrines.

So what can we offer instead of this Egypto-Syriac conglomeration? Fortunately there is a perfectly good explanation of the words on the triangle, using only the Hebrew language – an explanation that cannot be faulted in any way, and here it is.

The first syllable indicates eternal existence, the continuing and never-ending I AM. The second syllable, as we are told later (unfortunately only as an alternative) really does mean in Hebrew, "in heaven" or "on high" and the third syllable is a Hebrew word for Strength or Power.

Thus we do not need to go into apologies for faulty scholarship in the past, and we can leave Syria and Egypt and Chaldaea out of it altogether; for what we are pronouncing are not three names of God (or worse still the names of three gods, as some would suggest) but we are pronouncing three aspects or qualities of the Deity which are well known and well used, in Christianity and in other religions, namely His Eternal Existence, His Transcendence, and His Omnipotence. In other words we are describing The True and Living God – Most High – Almighty. It is as simple as that.

Unfortunately there are many printed rituals which still refer to the letters on the triangle as a name and not as a word. The Methodist committee evidently have such a copy, for their report says: "It has been suggested to us that this word is a *description* of God, but the ritual refers to the word as the *name* of God". With such evidence it is hard to see how they could conclude otherwise. But there are many other rituals which stress that the circle contains the name of God, and the triangle contains descriptive words. This is the explanation which, in my view, should be encouraged.

Now, I have been a mason long enough to know that nothing that is done in another Lodge or Chapter can be described as "wrong", it can only be described as "different". I am sure that when our ritual was revised in 1836 it all made perfectly good sense to those who revised it. Whether it still makes sense today is a matter of opinion, for there are so many "differences" that the situation has become absurd. In our Province alone we have twenty-one different Chapters with twenty-two different workings!

Has the time come when a new revision is due? Next year will be the one hundred and fiftieth anniversary of the last revision, and it might be more expedient for us to initiate such a revision ourselves, rather than have it forced on us by pressure from within and without: for there is no doubt that the continued reference to the word on the triangle as *a name* will bring us into disrepute with the world outside, and will cause an increase in the misgiving which already exists among our own members.

It is for this reason that I beg leave to draw your attention to my Alternative View of an entirely Hebrew interpretation which emphasises our reverence for

God whose sacred and mysterious Name is inscribed on the circle, while the triangle proclaims Him in no uncertain terms as "The True and Living God – The Most High – The Almighty".

Appendix X

TWO EXTRACTS FROM LETTERS FROM EX-MASONS

1   For a long time, even after my conversion, I defended masonry, and maintained that I was able to reconcile its philosophy and precepts – supposedly based on teaching morality and charity – with Christianity.

But in His time, and in His own gentle way, the Holy Spirit began to show me how blind I had been, and how effectively the enemy can use his weapons of subtlety and rationality in the blinding process. It was to the point of having my eyes fully open, and my heart sufficiently convicted of the evils attaching to masonry and the powerful bondage it imposes. It was one of the hardest things I have ever had to do – getting rid of my regalia, masonic literature and all the outward trappings of this evil craft. But this was not enough – the Holy Spirit showed that another step had to be taken in order to completely release me from the bondage I was in, and that was to approach a brother in Christ who would pray for my release. This he did, with the laying on of hands.

What a beautiful sense of lightness and freedom I experienced when that oppression was lifted!

2   A young man in his early forties confided in me recently about obscene sexual images that he was having during his times of spiritual communion, as well as disturbing feelings about blood and killing loved ones. This man is stable, mature, and has no history of mental illness. After counselling it was discovered that the sexual imagery was linked to Freemasonry symbols, the blood and the knife which he was tempted to use to kill a loved one was linked with the Oaths in Freemasonry. When this man was cut free from all his links with Freemasonry in the name of Jesus those very disturbing feelings and images went and he has not been troubled since.

Select Bibliography

Books and Leaflets supplied by the United Grand Lodge:

i)   *Constitutions of the Antient Fraternity of Free and Accepted Masons under the United Grand Lodge of England*, U.G.L. of E. 1984 (including Supreme Grand Chapter Regulations and Grand Charity Constitutions and Regulations).

ii)   *Information for the Guidance of Members of the Craft*. U.G.L. of E. 1985.

iii) *Freemasonry – From Craft to tolerance*. Text of a talk given by Commander M.B.S. Higham RN in St Margaret Pattens Church, Eastcheap, October 1985.

iv)   *Report of the Committee of Enquiry under Mr Justice Bagnall*. December 1973.

v)   *Information on Masonic Charities*. Masonic Charities 1983.

vi)   *The Grand Charity*. Council of Grand Charity 1985.

vii) *The Government of the Craft – A Prestonian Lecture 1982* by Sir James Stubbs KCVO. 1981.

viii) *The Craft: A History of English Freemasonry*, John Hamill. Crucible 1986.

ix)   Leaflet: *What is Freemasonry*. Board of General Purposes, October 1984.

x)   Leaflet: *Freemasonry and Religion*. Board of General Purposes, December 1985.

xi)   Leaflet: *What Every Candidate Should Know*. U.G.L. of E.

Freemasonry – A Way of Salvation?, The Revd John Lawrence. Grove Books 1985.

Freemasonry – A Religion, The Revd John Lawrence. Kingsway Publications 1987.

Emulation Ritual. Lewis (Masonic Publishers) Ltd., 7th edition 1985.

Darkness Visible: A Christian Appraisal of Freemasonry, Walton Hannah. Augustine Publishing Co. 1984.

Christian by Degrees: The non-Christian nature of Masonic Ritual, Walton Hannah. Augustine Publishing Co. 1984.

The Brotherhood: The Secret World of the Freemasons, Stephen Knight. Granada Publishing Ltd. 1984.

Report of the Faith and Order Committee of the Methodist Conference, 1985.

Report of Proceedings of the Church Assembly, vol. xxxi, 1951.

General Synod, February Group of Sessions 1985, *Report of Proceedings*. CIO Publishing.

Should a Christian be a Freemason? Andy Arbuthnot. The London Healing Mission.